EDWARDIAN
Children

JOANNA SMITH

EDWARDIAN
Children

HUTCHINSON
LONDON MELBOURNE SYDNEY AUCKLAND JOHANNESBURG

Hutchinson & Co. (Publishers) Ltd
An imprint of the Hutchinson Publishing Group
17 –21 Conway Street, London W1P 6JD

Hutchinson Group (Australia) Pty Ltd
30 –32 Cremorne Street, Richmond South, Victoria 3121
PO Box 151, Broadway, New South Wales 2007

Hutchinson Group (NZ) Ltd
32 –34 View Road, PO Box 40-086, Glenfield, Auckland 10

Hutchinson Group (SA) Pty Ltd
PO Box 337, Bergvlei 2012, South Africa

First published 1983
© Joanna Smith 1983

Set in VIP Cheltenham Book by D. P. Media Ltd,
Hitchin, Hertfordshire

Printed in Great Britain by W. S Cowell Ltd, London and Ipswich
and bound by Anchor Brendon Ltd

British Library Cataloguing in Publication Data
Smith, Joanna
    Edwardian children.
    1. Children—Great Britain—History
    20th century 2. Great Britain—Social
    life and customs—20th century
    I. Title
    941.082'3   HQ792.G7

ISBN 0 09 147910 X

CONTENTS

SOURCES

HOP-PICKING: THE TRADITIONAL
HOLIDAY FOR FAMILIES FROM THE EAST
END OF LONDON

The quotations which form so large a part of this book are taken, in almost every case, from the author's tape recordings of conversations with people who grew up before and during the First World War. Some inaccuracy and distortion there must be in the spoken word, but in compensation there is the freshness of memories which have risen naturally to the surface of the mind and which have not been checked, labelled and arranged for a written memoir.

The people who have talked to me about their childhood are listed, with brief details of their early lives where these would be helpful to the reader. I am most grateful to them all for their help and interest.

Miss Theresa Cox: born in County Sligo in 1894; went into service at the age of twelve and remained in service until she retired at seventy-five.

Mrs Victoria Dane: born in Cairo in 1899; the daughter of Sir Reginald Wingate, (one of the most distinguished of a military family which includes Orde Wingate of the Chindits) Governor General of the Sudan from 1899 to 1917. She was brought up in Khartoum and in Scotland and is Queen Victoria's last surviving god-daughter.

The Dowager Duchess of Devonshire: Lady Mary Cecil, born 1895. Her father was the fourth Marquess of Salisbury, the Conservative statesman; her grandfather, the third Marquess, was prime minister until he resigned in 1902. She lived in London and at Hatfield House, Hertfordshire.

Sir William Fellowes: born 1899; educated at Winchester College.

Miss Elizabeth Franks: born in London 1887; worked as a milliner from the age of fourteen.

Mrs Grizel Hartley: daughter of Sir George Seaton Buchanan, an expert on public health. Lived in Chiswick; educated at St Paul's Girls' School, London, where Gustav Holst was director of music from 1905 onwards.

Miss Catherine Harvie: born in Motherwell, Scotland; daughter of an engineer; became a nanny after training in Edinburgh.

Mrs Mabel Huxley: born in Ashford, Kent, in 1886; one of the ten children of a shop manager.

The Hon. Mrs Richard Lyttelton: Judith Clive, daughter of Captain Clive, soldier and MP for South Herefordshire; lived at Whitfield in Herefordshire.

Mr Charles Mitchell: born and brought up in Cardiff, the son of a baker.

Mrs Dora Orr: born in London 1899; daughter of a quail merchant; orphaned at the age of four; brought up in a convent orphanage, Aberdeen.

Mr Frank Rattey: born in Winchester 1896; after leaving school sold newspapers; was later apprenticed to a whitesmith; joined the army in 1914; served in India and Mesopotamia.

Miss Dora Rees: born near Swansea 1888; educated at Christ's Hospital for Girls; became a teacher.

The Dowager Lady Remnant: born in India; daughter of Lt-Col. A. J. Wogan-Browne, of the Indian Cavalry. Came to England 1905, brought up in Ascot by her grandmother Mrs Primrose, widow of General Primrose, defender of Kandahar in the Third Afghan War.

Mrs Catherine Staples: born 1892; daughter of the architect Frederick Hyde Pownall. Lived in Twickenham.

Mr Thomas Talbot: author's father. Born 1905; son of a barrister; lived in Wilton Crescent, London, and in Kent. Educated Summerfields, Oxford, and Winchester College.

Mrs Mabel Walker: born in Fraserburgh, Scotland 1901; daughter of a brewer; educated in Fraserburgh and Aberdeen.

I have also drawn on the unpublished memoirs of my great-aunt, Lady Stephenson (Gwendolen Talbot) and of Leila, Viscountess Hampden; I have also quoted from published memoirs and from magazines, periodicals and books of the day.

The sources of the illustrations are credited on page 188. Many come from private albums belonging to my parents and others; they are reproduced thanks to the generosity of their owners and the expertise of Harold Chapman, who photographed the albums with all the care due to their age and fragility.

INTRODUCTION

CAMBORNE TROLLEY BUS

In Cheltenham there is a statue of Edward VII: a ragged child stands trustfully, close to the Emperor King, the latter clad in marble plus-fours and lovingly textured marble socks and brogues. Ambrose Neale, the sculptor, intended it to represent 'King Edward as the Spirit of Peace leading the Spirit of Mischief to the Still Waters'; an appropriate symbol of the reign. The rags are there, but so is the benevolent king. The Edwardian decade, sandwiched between the appalling poverty of the nineteenth century and the horrors of the Great War, seems a golden age; the poverty was still there, but attempts were being made to alleviate it and England was a land of hope as well as of glory.

Through the eyes and voices of those who were children before 1914 I have tried to re-create something of the flavour of their everyday lives, avoiding the extremes of rich and poor – judging those, however, by the standards of the day. The word Edwardian can conjure up an opulent vulgarity – a whiff of cigar smoke, gargantuan meals, Parma violets and champagne – or scenes of seamy back streets and rural slums. Slums and opulence existed, but so did the comfortable life of prosperous Edwardian families, a way of life that has vanished utterly except in the memories of

NANNIES IN HAMPSTEAD

people now in their seventies and eighties. It lingered on, oddly, in books written for children, who took in their stride pages full of maids, nannies, governesses, ponies and hunting, manor houses and moated granges, long after these things had almost ceased to be.

It was a life of unsophisticated treats and pleasures, calm and secure. 'Everything was stable,' recalled my great-aunt, 'the background made by an army of servants, friendly to us and a social unit in themselves. We always said that we were poor, but that never really cramped everyday life; there was always a great deal of food and coal fires everywhere and open house for anyone we wanted to invite.' Often, as the children of those Edwardian years grew up, their stable, ordered homes seemed dull and restricted. They might rebel against family prayers; unmarried daughters might yearn for an independent role. ('Too old to obey,' my father heard an aunt resentfully mutter.) But three-quarters of a century later, it is easier to value the security and self-confidence which were swept away for ever in 1914.

Chapter One
THE NURSERY

BABY

'I THINK EVERYONE LOVED THEIR
NANNY MORE THAN THEIR MOTHER'

NANNY, MOTHER AND CHILD

I think everyone loved their nanny more than their mother;
that was certainly true of me. They were such wonderful
nannies, such personalities. And parents were so much more
aloof, and often away.

Edwardian children lived at a distance from their parents.
The nursery was generally at the very top of the house, as
remote as possible from the adult life below, and there Nanny
was the absolute, and generally benevolent, despot. This was not
always a happy arrangement. Leila Hampden, whose mother died
when she and her brother were very small, recalls Nanny Jones:

She frequently lost her temper, and would then beat us with a large flat
wooden paper knife ornamented with ducks. Her faults were obvious, and
I believe my mother was about to sack her when she died. . . . We argued
with each other as to whether Nanny was or was not a witch and we
decided that she *was*: her coal black hair, not all on her head, decided
matters.

But in very many families, loving nannies forged a bond with the
children that was broken only by death:

When Nanny came to us [said Judith Lyttelton] she'd been having £10 a
year and my mother said, 'I'm going to give you £16.' Nanny said she
couldn't believe that *anyone* got £16 a year. She stayed with us until she
died, and she was paid – I don't know what exactly, but the equivalent of
£16; it couldn't have been much, because that was a long time ago. When
she died she left my sister £3000. So when I engaged a nanny and she said,
'I never go out, Mrs Lyttelton; not *for the first year*' – well, I took it for
granted of course that she wouldn't, because my nanny *never* went out.

The mother's first duty was to her husband, who might well be
building the Empire, or defending it in the armed forces, or making
his way in his profession, but Nanny was always there, a stable and
loving presence. It was the nanny who sat with the children when
they were ill, made them blackcurrant tea, or prepared a camphorated oil compress.

A lovely thing was that hot compress, with camphorated oil, on the chest.
Oh, the comfort of it, if you had a really bad cold. You had a great lump of
cotton wool, which had been warmed up in front of the fire, and the
camphorated oil was warmed as well.

Every nanny had her own favourite remedies. Leila Hampden's
Nanny Chivers, who succeeded the infamous Nanny Jones, was 'a
good fairy to us all, in spite of dosing us every Saturday with
loathsome Syrup of Figs, and squirting our noses with Glyco-
Thymoline whenever we had colds'. Other medicines were
'Gregory Powder, quite dreadful' and 'quinine for colds, not the
ammoniated but the tincture. It was more revolting than words can

'FIRST THE INFANT . . . IN ITS MOTHER'S
ARMS' (JESSIE WILCOX SMITH, 1908)

tell you – wonderful if you've got malaria, but we didn't have malaria. I don't know where she got the idea from or if it was any good.'

The nanny took entire charge of a child from the moment that it was weaned. She would bath it in a baby bath, 'round and solid like a Norman font'.

If you went into any mother's or child's room, all you could see was the behind of the nanny, washing the baby in the bath. And there was the lovely smell of hot paint from the brown hot-water cans. The nursery maids brought up all these enormous brown cans for our baths; they must have held two gallons at least. Up they came, up the back stairs. We had baths in front of the fire in the nursery; one was a hip bath and one was shaped like a coffin. It was divine.

It was rare indeed to have a bathroom on the nursery floor; every drop of water was carried up and down stairs by the maids, who would also clean the nurseries, light the fires, carry up the coal and bring up the nursery meals. If there was a nursery maid under the

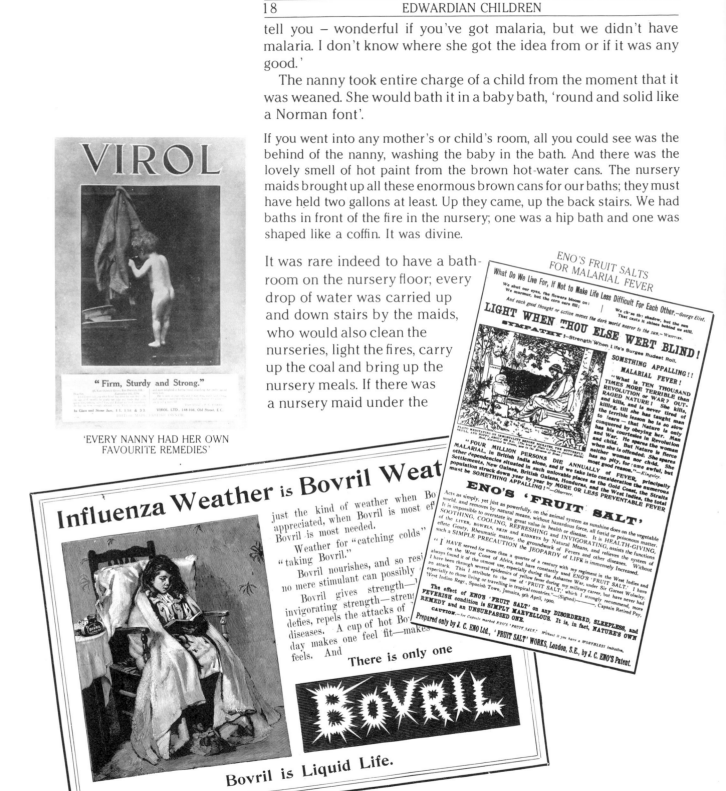

VIROL

"Firm, Sturdy and Strong."

VIROL LTD., 148-166, Old Street, E.C.

'EVERY NANNY HAD HER OWN FAVOURITE REMEDIES'

ENO'S FRUIT SALTS FOR MALARIAL FEVER

ENO'S 'FRUIT SALT'

Prepared only by J. C. ENO Ltd., 'FRUIT SALT' WORKS, London, S.E., by J. C. ENO'S Patent.

Influenza Weather is Bovril Weat[her]

There is only one

BOVRIL

Bovril is Liquid Life.

BOVRIL FOR A SICK CHILD

'ONE WAS SHAPED LIKE A COFFIN'

A BATH IN FRONT OF THE FIRE

nanny, she would do these tasks and also help with the children, washing and drying them and mending their clothes. If Nanny trusted the nursery maid and if the children were well, she might go down to the servants' hall for supper, where there was

a tremendous ritual. They had beef and beer, and then after the meat course, which was eaten in silence, the upper servants – the butler, the housekeeper, the lady's maid, the head housemaid, the cook and the nurse – would sweep out to the housekeeper's room and there they would indulge in a bottle of port.

The nursery, however, was the room where both nanny and children spent most of their time. It would have a large sturdy table in the middle, used for meals and games and a high brass fender around the fire, on which the children's clothes were aired. Apart from the cheerful fire, nurseries were often somewhat spartan. The floors were usually covered with linoleum; this was considered hygienic, particularly for the night-nurseries. Or there might be a carpet, dark grey or brown, made probably of indestructible and scratchy hardcord.

Toys were few and Christmas presents, according to many accounts, 'extremely feeble'. 'The only toy I can remember having was a wooden horse on wheels, and I loved it,' said Dora Orr. 'The legs fell off and in the end there was only the body left. I put it under my arm and carried it wherever I went.' Teddy bears and golliwogs were new arrivals in the nursery. Golliwogs were invented by Florence K. Upton; the first in her series of 'Golliwogg' books appeared in 1895. Teddy bears owed their name to President Theodore Roosevelt, but English children detected a resemblance to their monarch. 'The King was known as Teddy, and Teddy bears, which came in about this time and were very popular, as they still

THE NURSERY FENDER ON WHICH THE
CLOTHES WERE AIRED
(POSTCARD, 1911)

A BUBBLE PIPE (POSTCARD, 1907)

BUILDING BRICKS

SELLING CHRISTMAS TOYS

are, we all firmly believed to have been called after the King.' King
Edward was associated with at least one other toy, as my father
remembers: 'When King Edward died, the tabloid press was very
keen on his terrier, Caesar, who attended the funeral procession.
And there were sold, and I had one, toy dogs with a medal round
their necks which said "I am Caesar, the King's Own Dog". '

After tea the nursery children would go down to the drawing
room. 'That was the only time really you saw your parents.' They
were first dressed in clean clothes. 'I was put into a linen frock,
which I very much disliked,' said my father. 'I didn't like the feeling
of warm linen, I don't know why.'

Board games might be played in the drawing room. These were
often topical; the new scout movement gave birth to *Scouting*, in a
suitably uplifting format; *The Aerial Derby* and *The Game of Motor-
ing* kept Edwardian children abreast of modern developments, and
there were also 'educational' games such as *Word Making, Word
Taking*, and *Answerit*, a kind of quiz on cards in which bright

THE AUTHOR'S MOTHER WITH HER
DOLL.

THE QUEEN MOTHER, DRESSED FOR THE DRAWING ROOM

A FAMILY IN 1907

children could answer such questions as 'Q: What is the capital of Russia? A: St Petersburg.'

A magic lantern might be produced and its coloured glass pictures projected by the aid of a candle in the little metal box behind the slides:

I can still smell the pungent smell of the oil lamps and see the waving slides, very often upside down. There was one missionary lecture in the village school when the patient lecturer, having struggled with many unwanted slides, bravely pointed to the watch-chain across the middle of a more than life-size bishop and said 'We will call *this* the Zambezi River. . . .'

Another treat was peering at double photographs through a stereoscopic viewer which gave a three-dimensional effect.

You looked through this thing, and you could see the lovely house with the family, and the palms on the piano, and everything. My father had a set on the Boer War, but we weren't so interested in that.

'NANNY SAT IN THE DONKEY CART WITH THE CHILDREN.' NANNY COSTER ('COSSIE') WITH THE AUTHOR'S FATHER AND HIS BROTHER AND SISTER

Nanny was the leader of the children's expeditions. In the country, she sat in the donkey cart with the children and drove the sun-hatted donkey, or she might even find herself in charge of a goat:

Goats never get TB so it was settled that all the poor and everybody in the surrounding villages should have goats. So we at one time bred goats, and we had the most dreadful billygoat. They're very fierce, billygoats, and one day it got loose and attacked the housekeeper. It was terrible, but I think she was all right; she didn't die or anything. But we also had a darling nanny goat we drove in the goat cart, which was white and green basket-work and would now at Christie's be selling for a fortune.

A RIDE ON A HORSE-DRAWN BUS

'ONE OF THE RATHER INFREQUENT MOTOR BUSES'

Less adventurously, in London, the nanny might take the children to the zoo on a horse-drawn bus, or better still, a motor bus. 'When my sister was ill, Cossie [the nanny] was nursing her and we had a temporary nanny. And we were able to prevail upon her to wait for one of the rather infrequent motor buses; Cossie would never have let us do that.' More exciting still were the serialized silent movies at the Electric Palace at Marble Arch, where jerky figures in a perpetual scratchy snowstorm worked their way through an increasingly improbable and melodramatic plot, week by week, to a piano accompaniment. In the intervals, the audience was sprayed by the elderly usherettes 'with what we thought was wonderful scent, but it was in fact some kind of disinfectant'.

For some children these early days were among the most exciting and vivid of their lives – those whose parents were abroad, in the East or in Africa. Victoria Dane's father was governor of the Sudan, and until she was six she lived in General Gordon's palace in Khartoum, 'an enormous palace with great marble verandahs all the way round and the steps on which Gordon was killed'. In her case a nanny was replaced by a nursery governess, whose job it was to do some elementary teaching as well as to look after her:

dear Miss Snelling, whom I adored. I was the only white child in the Sudan so she had to teach me a certain amount. Once, we were going through the Bay of Biscay and it was terribly rough; I was about five and I kept thinking, 'What will happen when the ship sinks?' So I said, 'Miss Snelling, when the ship sinks, do you think the fishes will eat our souls, or would the leather be too tough?' I imagined, you see, that in the middle of one's body was a soul, made out of leather, like the sole of a shoe.

Victoria Dane was born in Cairo:

Father, you see, was just fighting a battle. I was born a fortnight early because poor Mother was so agitated about Father fighting this battle. Then Father arrived. I was going to be called Lesley because my grandmother on my mother's side was a Lesley. Then suddenly, owing to this battle being won, mostly by Father I think, a thing arrived from Queen Victoria to say that 'Her Majesty wishes to be sponsor to your daughter; she is to be called Victoria Alexandrina'. And that was that.

In those days the only people who came to the Sudan were very rich people, for hunting parties and that sort of thing. They hunted lion and elephant and my father would give them permission. Archaeologists came, but my mother would never have a scarab or anything like that. She had the idea that people shouldn't disturb the bodies of the dead. They had been put there with great ceremony, with food to eat and everything for the after-life, and she couldn't bear the idea of their bodies being moved. She would never have anything, herself, that was out of a tomb, because she disapproved terribly of it.

My parents were very interested in the archaeology and the people who came to dig. Many, many years ago, when they were opening the tombs of

GLASGOW TRAM

the kings in Egypt, I was a small child. There's a photograph of me somewhere in a large topee going down to see the tombs of the kings. I remember it so well. I was taken to see the tomb of Rameses II, and the mummy was there, all uncovered. My nursery governess was with me; I was about five or six – something like that. I said, 'But he's asleep! That can't be anybody dead, he's asleep!' The mummy, which had just been unwrapped, was absolutely perfect, you couldn't believe it. It's now, I think, in the museum in Cairo.

After the age of five or six it was considered too dangerous to allow young children to stay in the East; the risks to health were too great. So the children left for England to be brought up, often by an aunt or a grandmother, and they might not see their father again for some years, and their mother only at long intervals. Victoria Dane remembers her last day in Khartoum:

My mother could never make it out; she said to my father, 'Victoria must have Gordon ingrained in her mind, because whenever we go home she always wants to go to the Gordon statue to say goodbye to Gordon – isn't it extraordinary? She thinks about Gordon all the time.' However, the last time, when I was about six – that was the last time that I was allowed to go out to Khartoum – I went to say goodbye to Gordon; we drove out in the victoria, and I said to my mother, 'Mother, who is the funny little man riding dear Gordon?' You see, the statue was of Gordon riding a beautiful camel, with all the trappings and so on, and I thought that the *camel* was dear Gordon.

Even for children in England health was a major preoccupation. 'Edwardians were great believers in fresh air. They thought you would die unless you had your bedroom window open at night. And you would also die if you didn't walk at least three miles a day.' There were all the normal childhood diseases; these included diphtheria and whooping cough and

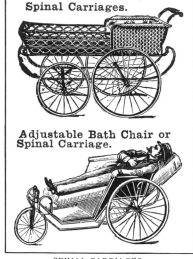

Spinal Carriages.

Adjustable Bath Chair or Spinal Carriage.

SPINAL CARRIAGES

of course, there was tuberculosis in those days, very much so. That you did hear about. I don't know that I ever saw anyone dying of it but you were aware of all the TB sanatoriums.

I led rather a solitary life, in a way [said Grizel Hartley], because my brother developed tuberculosis, and my mother was determined to get him right. She thought it was all her fault for living in London. He had tuberculosis of the spine, which nearly always was a killer in those days, or else you came out a total cripple. He was only three years old. My mother was determined to get him right, and get him right she did. She took him to Broadstairs, and she lived with him, absolutely out-of-doors, for three or four years. All the winters, she said, she never saw anyone but the lamplighter and the coast guard; my brother was in a spinal carriage and she tried to keep herself warm, and tried to keep him warm. The result was that not only was he perfectly all right, but he played rugby football for Sandhurst. It was a kind of miracle really. The great thing is, if you've got tuberculosis of the spine, never to move and she was terribly good at seeing that he never moved.

In 1907 *Bibby's Annual* commented that 'At the present time there is no power to stop the sale of the milk of a tuberculous cow, unless there exists tubercular disease of the udder.' Parents and nannies were understandably nervous. Sometimes the milk was boiled, or the children were made to drink goat's milk. Ice cream vendors were common but 'we certainly weren't allowed to buy ice cream'.

MOTHERS WITH THEIR BABIES AT THE INFANTS' HOSPITAL

INFANTS' HOSPITAL, VINCENT SQUARE, LONDON

'YOU WERE AWARE OF ALL THE TB SANATORIUMS'

A WARD IN THE ALEXANDRA HOSPITAL FOR CHILDREN WITH HIP DISEASES

'PEOPLE HAD A SPRING, OR A FILTER;
ONE OR THE OTHER'

Water was another problem. 'We had a special pump, with spring water. We weren't allowed to drink pond water; that would have been the *end*! People had a spring, or a filter; one or the other.'

Any train journey usually involved fleas:

When we arrived, Cossie [the nanny] would detect flea bites, and with the help of the nursery maid she would hunt through my vest for the flea and there was a hue and cry when it was spotted. It was run to earth – or wool – and nipped between Cossie's thumb and forefinger. There were no lice; fleas were the worst and you certainly expected to pick them up if you travelled third-class to Norfolk. For some reason fleas were less in evidence on the London, Brighton and South Coast Railway. I never recall picking up fleas on the way to Kent.

Flea hunting must have been made more difficult by the elaborate clothes that everyone wore. Babies were dressed in beautiful

long dresses, trimmed with lace, tucked and smocked and rib-
boned. The nannies would take the children shopping for stuffs and
ribbons, measured out on a brass rule set in the shop counter, for
making and trimming their clothes. Nobody, however young or old,
went out without a hat. Babies wore elaborate bonnets; little girls
wide shady hats; boys wore sailor hats.

We used to go to a shop, Peter Yapp I think it was called, in Sloane Street,
where there were splendid sailor hats with a ribbon round them which
said HMS *Victory*; there was also a star on the top, no doubt as worn in the
Royal Navy. However, my mother thought it vulgar to have an HMS *Victory*

'BABIES WORE ELABORATE BONNETS'

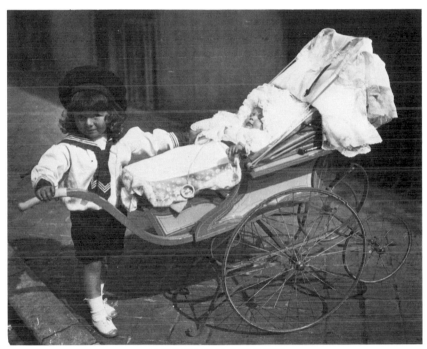

'BOYS WORE SAILOR HATS'

THE AUTHOR'S MOTHER IN HER
PETTICOAT

ribbon, so it was always changed for a black ribbon, which I thought very
inferior, and the little star on the top was taken off; I was always bitterly
disappointed.

The hats were kept on by elastic under the chin. 'Elastic kept on
any hat, even in a high wind. Sometimes the elastic broke and so
when my brother saw a picture of St Peter with a halo his comment
was "He's lost his elastic!" '

The nursery was a closed world and even older children in the
family were, up to a point, excluded from its secure familiarity in
the same way that they were excluded from other parts of the
house. 'The nursery was the nursery, and the schoolroom was the
schoolroom. You went to the drawing room only after tea and the
housekeeper's room by invitation as a treat.'

'GIRLS WORE SHADY HATS'

'NOBODY, HOWEVER YOUNG OR OLD, WENT OUT WITHOUT A HAT'

THE NURSERY

If now that seems formal, cold and strange, children today might none the less envy the security of the nursery world and the loving and undivided attention of a good nanny. In most Edwardian nurseries, the last sounds heard by the sleepy children were comforting and familiar ones; the grown-ups talking to each other as they went downstairs after dressing for dinner, the scrape of the chairs as they sat down to the table, 'and there was always Nanny in the nursery'.

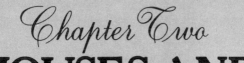

Chapter Two

HOUSES AND HOUSEHOLDS

THE FOURTEEN SERVANTS OF A RATHER
MODEST COUNTRY HOUSE

BREAKFAST, 1905

A FAMILY AT LUNCH

I found a diary of my mother's, in which she wrote: 'I think I can manage with a cook, a kitchen maid, two housemaids, four gardeners and my maid. It will be a struggle – but I think I can manage.

Her ladyship was very good, very kind and everybody liked her, but she *would* come in to the kitchen sometimes and say to the cook, 'Well, you're going to have a holiday today because the Captain and I are out for lunch and dinner, so that will be a complete rest for you, won't it?', quite ignoring the fact that there were ten in the nursery and fifteen in the servants' hall!

A large country house was a whole world:

There was no question of being lonely, there were so many servants and retainers. There were three in the kitchen, three in the house and three in the pantry; then Nanny and the nurserymaid and my mother's maid. That was twelve in the house. Outside there were ten gardeners, and originally there were five people working in the laundry, but I can only just remember those. Then there were the grooms and the coachman in the stables, and the farm, with a lovely dairy. And of course there were the gamekeepers, at least three or four of them, the head keeper, and the forestry workers. There must have been fifty people, or even more.

It was a tremendous hierarchy:

You had the butler, and in very large houses you had a sort of palace steward who was incredibly grand. Then there was the housekeeper, the cook, the lady's maid and the valet. The butler used to join the others just for the pudding. At a shoot the keeper had to be given two bottles of whisky, one for himself and one to offer around. The lady's maids used to put out their shoes to be cleaned and they were far more particular than the ladies. The steps had to be whitened every day by a housemaid and if it wasn't done properly the housekeeper would throw ink on the step and say, 'Do it again.' Some housekeepers were real tyrants.

THE HOUSEMAID: A PUZZLE PICTURE FROM THE CHILDREN'S ENCYCLOPAEDIA
WHAT IS WRONG IN THIS ROOM?

This picture has been drawn with seventeen things wrong in it. It will interest you to find out these mistakes and write them down, comparing your list with the correct list appearing on page 3285.

'WHEN YOU WERE MAKING SOUP FOR THE POOR, IT WASN'T WORTH MAKING LESS THAN THREE GALLONS'

Even the poor families on the estate had large households – 'I mean, when you were making soup for the poor it wasn't worth making less than three gallons' – while the poorer gentry and very unpretentious middle-class families employed a considerable number of people. 'I really don't know how many servants my mother had. You see their wages were only half a crown a week,' said Mabel Walker, while Lady Remnant remembers:

In my grandmother's house – and after all, she wasn't well off, she was a soldier's widow – there was a housemaid, parlourmaid, cook and gardener. The gardener also looked after the dogcart and the horse, which my grandmother drove herself. No widow of a soldier could live like that now.

Servants were considered a necessity, not a luxury, by any family which could conceivably afford them, because the physical effort of running a house without electricity or plumbing was enormous. This was washday in a Scottish home before the First War:

Oh my dear, the washing! We had Lizzie come in to do the washing. And every Sunday either the housekeeper or I had to go down with all the dirty linen. We had to soak it – that was most important, to soak your washing the night before. Then we set the fire, one of those fires where you put the washing in the boiler, which was a great stone thing, and a copper. So the fire was all laid, ready to be hot for the washerwoman, and then early in the morning the housekeeper went in to light the fire to heat the water for her. I think she came about eight, Lizzie. She was a dear old girl and she stayed with us for years and years. Every Monday morning she came. She had her breakfast nine-ish and then she had her lunch before she went. All the washing was done by this time, in the washhouse; terrific steam and

'HER FIRST WASHING-DAY'
(POSTCARD, 1908)

all done with soap on a board, rubbing it like blazes; then the old-fashioned mangle and out it went.

Now if it was a wet day, of course, Lizzie went up with a basket to the loft, and everything was hung up there. Then, when I was older I had to get up to the loft and bring the clothes down. Everything was starched – tablecloths, aprons, caps and dresses, and you had to damp them all, ready for the ironing. It was quite a palaver, I can assure you. Then they had to be ironed with the flatirons, which you had to put on the range, to make them hot. The gas irons came in, not long afterwards. They had a gas flame inside the iron. But you got accustomed to the flatirons. You had to have an ironing pad on your hands, but they really ironed beautifully.

Heating was all by coal and, in the country, log fires. The wood had to be felled, cut, stacked and brought into the house. Coal fires had to be cleaned out, blacked, laid, lit; coal scuttles had to be filled and carried into every room. Everywhere there was a coal fire burning.

Coal was twelve shillings a ton on the Welsh borders. It took George and the cart horse two days to collect the coal, because the station was two hours away. There was unlimited wood, lovely log fires. But cold. My God, it was cold – the passages. I remember how as a child, when you went down to the library at five o'clock, you really did shudder through the passages. You were either very cold, or very hot, it made you very resilient.

We cooked by the fire; everything was cooked by coal and we didn't have any electricity. I remember the new kitchen range coming. It was called an Eagle and it was huge and black and the last word – everyone had to have an Eagle range, it was the thing. There was no electric light;

THE PHYSICAL EFFORT OF RUNNING A HOUSE

A KITCHEN RANGE

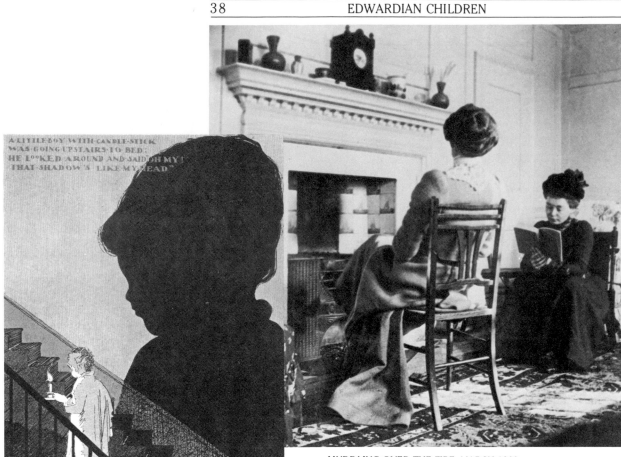

HUDDLING OVER THE FIRE, MARCH 1903

TAKING A CANDLE UP TO BED

we had oil lamps. A dear man called Ted had a large room, which was pitch dark, in the basement. That was his job, to look after the lamps. It took a long time to clean all the lamps for a big house. But of course they were marvellously warming, one forgets about that. Then when we went to bed we took a candle, not a lamp. There were rows of silver candle-sticks sitting on a table. We used to read in bed by the light of this one candle.

The downstairs rooms were lit by oil lamps, not candles, in houses without gas. The oil lamps were never left in the rooms during the day; they were removed, cleaned and filled and brought into the rooms at dusk:

I remember that thrill of arriving for Christmas; we were decanted at the back door and it was about the time that the lamps were being lit – there would be twenty or thirty lamps already lit, waiting to be carried into the house and the smell was the quintessence of the Christmas holidays.

It was a continual labour to keep such houses clean and, at the end of the winter, spring cleaning was a necessary ritual. Covers and curtains were removed and washed; carpets were carried outside and the winter dust and ash were beaten out of them with wicker carpet beaters; the furniture was draped in dust sheets and the house was cleaned from attic to cellar. Finally, everything was put back in its place and the house, smelling of soap and beeswax, was ready for the summer.

A large country house was almost medieval in its self-sufficiency:

I can just remember the hothouse grapes, and those early strawberries that you kept in the greenhouse and were ripe for Easter. You had to feed your household all the year round; there was no frozen food, nothing like that, so it had to be fed and it was, marvellously. There were no shops near us. We even had our own laundry. My mother got rid of it, because it really was rather a nuisance, but I can remember going into it. It was enormous, with all the lovely machines; goffering irons for making those tiny pleats. There were certainly four or five people working there.

The kitchen was simply huge, with a great scullery on one side and a larder on the other side. It had a tiled floor, red tiles, and it was sanded – the kitchenmaid threw down sand before she cleaned the floor to scour it. The dining-room food was very good. My mother loved curing hams; she was famous for her cured hams. She cured them with treacle and saltpetre and the fat came out a pale, lovely brown. Breakfast, I can remember that marvellous sideboard at breakfast – grilled pheasant and tongue and always a fish, and always a ham. When we shot rabbits the rabbit skins were the perk of the scullery maid. She sold them, probably for sixpence! A fortune! A man came round to collect the skins.

Out of doors there were the gardeners. Victoria Dane remembers:

our head gardener, dear Baker. If ever people came to lunch on Sunday, or tea, Baker would appear, always in his beautiful tweed suit and his bowler hat, which he would take off to greet them. He never would allow anybody but himself to take people round the garden. Mother *never* was allowed, although she was a marvellous gardener. She never did anything except occasionally spud up a dandelion, but she knew the name and Latin name of every plant and was wonderful at laying out a garden and making it look lovely. But Baker would appear and take people round *his* garden.

Another memorable head gardener was

Mr Grimrod. He was the most terrific head gardener, and why he was thought to be so good was that although he dressed as a head gardener, always with a hat and a suit, he would take off his coat at a moment's notice and show the new boy how to dig. That was thought to be remarkable, because most head gardeners wouldn't be seen dead with a spade, or anything like that.

And the force of Mr Grimrod's character was such that although he had eleven children and lived in a three-bedroomed cottage, 'the room on the left was *his* and no child went in there. He was a character, and young gardeners liked coming to be trained by him.'

IN THE GARDEN – MAXFIELD PARRISH'S ILLUSTRATION FOR *THE GOLDEN AGE*, BY KENNETH GRAHAME

Less intimidating were the under-gardeners:

They were all our friends. They had a lovely bothy – at least they called it lovely – which was where they ate and kept their tools. It was on the north side of the wall, just at the entrance to the kitchen garden – absolutely pitch black. The boiler room was down below, with the boiler for the greenhouses. It was so warm and lovely and there was nearly always a coal fire. I can see it now, so cosy with the fire and the boiler, and a bench all round, where they sat and ate their sandwiches, cobwebs hanging in every direction. But every spade, hoe and shovel gleamed and was put away spotless every night. My father took the bothy in hand, he thought it was too grubby and old fashioned, and he was going to have it done up and painted. Of course, this got round, as everything does, and a deputation came to say 'Please leave it, we like it as it is,' and so nothing was done.

A GROUP OF LADIES GARDENING

All the under-gardeners did was dig, and weed, and rake the gravel:

I can hear the noise now. At the front of the house there was an expanse of gravel and every Saturday morning it was raked – and there was never a weed. The under-gardeners all had their cottages, all of which we visited, because they were our friends; Nanny used to push us miles round the drives. They each had at least half an acre, and a pig, and a marvellous garden of their own, so they lived very well. They must have come as young under-gardeners, possibly with ambitions, but there was no question of any of them rising to be in the greenhouse, or to be foremen, let alone head gardener. Today they would be more ambitious; they would want to get on. But of course there was no mobility then; there wasn't much choice. If you lived near a big house, you hoped to God you would be taken on either on the farm or the garden, or the stables, or the house, because if not, what?

The stable room smelt of leather and there was always a fire going:

By this time the coachman was becoming the chauffeur; it was just about the changeover. But he had been brought up as coachman, so he could always be groom. There was always a groom, always somebody in the stables. There was every variety of dogcart, governess cart, goat cart, victorias and carriages.

Even after the changeover, old training died hard. Lady Remnant took her car to a garage in Chelsea:

One day the manager of the garage said to me, 'Have you ever looked underneath your car? I assure you, it's as clean underneath as it is on top, and I've had all my staff up to look at it.' That was old Hoppy, the chauffeur, because, you see, he'd been a groom and he'd kept all the

'BY THIS TIME THE COACHMAN WAS
BECOMING THE CHAUFFEUR'

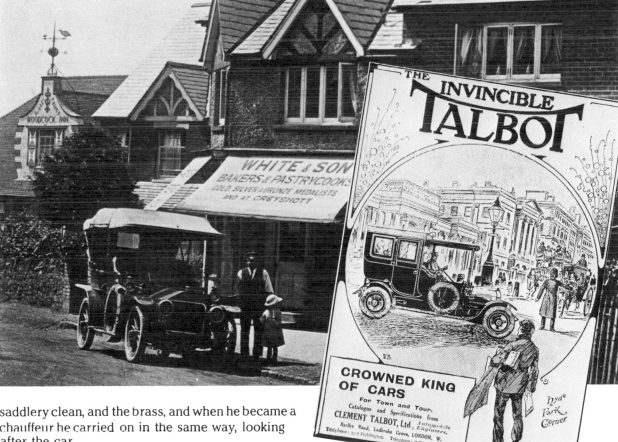

saddlery clean, and the brass, and when he became a chauffeur he carried on in the same way, looking after the car.

A CLEMENT TALBOT CAR

Not many cars were about before the First War: 'You wouldn't get ordinary normal people having a car before 1914. I had some American friends who had a car, but I don't remember any others.'... 'If you had a car you *had* to have a chauffeur. It sounds grand, but it was an absolute necessity,' because every time the car went out there was an incident. 'Punctures loomed very large' on the country roads, which consisted of stones rammed down in a very rough cement which more or less held them together.

We had a car in 1905, a Clement Talbot. She was covered in brass and she lasted until about 1928 – a magnificent sight she was. You were very high up. She was the most difficult car to learn to drive on – the gears ground – but somehow she went about. The roads were so dusty; I can remember the white lines in the hedges where the dust blew up to and there it stopped and it was nice green hedge again. As you drove along terrified horses would bolt, and you nearly always ran over something, a dog or a hen.

'EVERY TIME THE CAR WENT OUT THERE WAS AN INCIDENT'

'PUNCTURES LOOMED VERY LARGE'

'YOU *HAD* TO HAVE A CHAUFFEUR'

THE DUSTY ROAD

MORRIS OXFORD CARS OUTSIDE THE COWLEY FACTORY, 1913

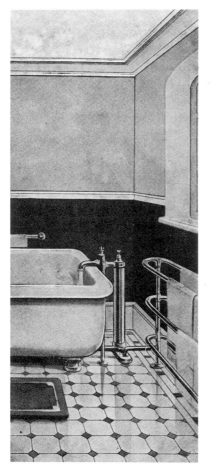

Less go-ahead houses had perhaps one or two bathrooms. 'We had two, one each end of the house, and people's maids and valets used to queue to get the bath for *their* lady or gentleman, before anyone else.'

Electricity was slow to reach the country. Here again Hatfield led the way:

It was so dangerous that in the gallery it used to catch fire. My grandfather put it in himself, which was quite wrong. He had lots of little lights in and out of the plaster ceiling, and quite often it would catch fire. And everyone used to take cushions and throw them at the ceiling to put it out. I think he was ahead of his time in a way. It was a long time before anyone else had electricity. It really was a miracle that the house wasn't burnt down. I think he was slightly conscious of it, because we had very regular fire drill. Great excitement! We got out of lessons. The footman and the house-maids all trundled to wherever they were supposed to be, and they used to unroll the pipes, which were kept rolled up all over the house. All we had were those very long pipes. I'm sure it would have been quite impossible to save the house. But all lessons were stopped, so it was always a day of rejoicing, fire drill day. We had a chute for getting out of the window. Very frightening; have you ever been down a chute? You go down feet first. There were a lot of stairs, luckily, so if there had been a fire and you couldn't get down one stairs you could get down another.

ELECTRIC TEAKETTLE, 1910

At my father's house there was a fire engine, horse-drawn, and a fire brigade. The head gardener was in charge; he had a rocket in his garden which he let off, if there was an alarm, to summon the firemen. It was taken extremely seriously, 'because if you had

THE PRIVATE FIRE BRIGADE AT THE AUTHOR'S FATHER'S HOUSE, 1907

waited for the fire brigade from Edenbridge – which was three miles away, and uphill – by the time the horse-drawn engine arrived your house would have been burned to ashes'. Every year a competition for the private fire brigades round about was held in the park; the firemen carried dummies down the ladders and aimed at a mark with jets of water from their hoses; the children practised descending from the nursery windows on a winch.

BRINGING DOWN THE DUMMY PERSON;
PRIVATE FIRE BRIGADES' COMPETITION,
1907

Such gala days apart, country children grew up in 'a deep quiet, where little treats were immensely enjoyed . . . tramps through the muddy lanes, cosy evenings of reading aloud, occasional visitors.' A strange face was seldom seen. 'That's a difference; you knew everybody. There was practically no traffic on what we called the High Road. There was dung all over the roads and the smallest roads were more or less mud, and not macadamized.' Travelling tinkers there were, and tramps; and you might see 'the roadmender sitting on his pile of stones, breaking them up with his pick'. In such isolation, children could and did have extraordinary freedom. It never occurred to anybody that they might be attacked or molested and of course there was no danger from traffic. 'Life was very free for children; simply glorious. Having got your button boots on and been carefully wrapped up, you were loose; no child came to harm then.'

'A DEEP QUIET'

A RIDE IN THE FARM CART

'LIFE WAS VERY FREE FOR CHILDREN'

Mabel Walker recalls:

We had a lot of freedom. I was allowed to do just what I liked. We used to walk out to my grandparents' farm, about two miles. And we used to swim naked; there was nobody there to see us. There were little rivers going to the sea, and we used to swim in those rivers – not boys, only girls of course, and we were only young, seven or eight years old perhaps. And I went fishing; I baited my own hooks and I caught lovely plaice and dabs, and lots of horrid eels. That was a lovely life, walking and fishing, and all the wild birds overhead, the teal and all the marsh birds – and not a soul but me.

Victoria Dane remembers:

I had my pony and you see in those days it was perfectly safe. I had a great friend who lived up on the moors, in an old farmhouse. She had a pony too, and it was eight miles away. I used to ride there on my pony. Nobody thought there was anything peculiar about it. I would ride up and spend the day with her, and I was told when I had to be home. It was perfectly safe, because there were practically no cars and they knew nobody would touch me.

Judith Lyttelton and her brother used to go out alone together in the donkey cart which was long and low and

had to be turned very subtly, or the front wheels locked into the back wheels. This donkey adored churches, and Herefordshire is littered with

'THERE WAS PRACTICALLY NO TRAFFIC'

LEANING OVER THE BRIDGE

churches. I think, possibly, it may have been fed at some church. So whenever the donkey saw a church, he made for the entrance and we were always getting stuck. Why we were allowed out in this cart by ourselves I don't know. My mother was very brave that way; she didn't mind what we did. She bought us these woolly ponies off the Welsh hills; they were cheap, mostly unbroken, and we had to collect them out of the field before hunting. And then we would fall about everywhere and all my mother ever said was, 'Get up, stop crying and remember you're a soldier's daughter.' And having hunted on our woolly pony and fallen off, it was quite easy to find ourselves ten or fifteen miles from home and we had to hack home. No one had ever heard of a horse box or anything like that. It was mostly raining – it always rains in Herefordshire – so we were wet through. When we came home there was usually somebody in the stables, but my mother always made us make sure that the pony was rubbed down before we came in to have some tea.

It was a life of freedom and self-reliance within a framework of discipline demanded by a large and smooth-running household. The children could roam freely all day, trapping moles or shooting rooks and come in covered with mud, but

there was this discipline behind it all. Absolute punctuality for meals. You could come in as dirty as you liked, but you changed and you came down to the drawing room at five o'clock, really dressed-up tidy. Absolute politeness all the time, especially to servants, because they couldn't answer back, you were told.

At Hatfield children were in and out all day and all evening and they had one rule – you must not interrupt your elders and betters. If you didn't interrupt you could come and go as you liked, so you jolly well learned

GETTING READY FOR POLO

THE STABLES: THE AUTHOR'S MOTHER
ON HER PONY

TEATIME

not to interrupt. From time to time a kindly guest would say, 'How are you getting on? And how are the horses?' My mother looked very pleased if a well-behaved daughter answered correctly.

Victoria Dane

always had prayers in the morning. We all filed in, servants, guests, everyone – they all had to appear. We used to kneel against the dining-room chairs and if you cast your eye around, all you could see were behinds. Everyone knelt with their faces to the wall and you could see a row of print dresses. It only lasted a few minutes, father would read part of the Litany. And I shall never forget the dreadful day when they said, 'Why were you not down for prayers?' By this time I was becoming rather independent and I said, 'I don't intend to come down for prayers if I don't wish to.' There was the most awful row over this.

Family prayers were for many an uncomfortable experience. My great-aunt, deeply religious though she was, found them thoroughly embarrassing:

'Prayers is ready,' the butler would rather strangely announce. The choosing of the unaccompanied hymn led to much controversy and a good deal of humming. I remember Lord Hugh Cecil trying to indicate the hymn of his choice with quite unrecognizable humming; I can see Ish and Ted getting uncontrollable giggles as, sharing a hymn book, they 'feathered for the bass' and Mrs Charles Furse's dismayed: 'Where are we going now?' as we headed off for the dining room, where the long row of servants already stood at attention ... to me, Sunday evening prayers were a weekly trial.

We went to church every Sunday, with a penny. One of my brothers used to leave his coat at the back of the church, so that he could keep his penny and not put it in the bag. Oh, we were very much hauled off, and it was a häul, because it was two miles' trudge through the wood, or three miles by road. We more often drove, because if we had walked we wouldn't have been very tidy.

It was quite common to go to church twice every Sunday, and have family prayers every morning before breakfast. There was a chaplain at Hatfield, and there was a service every morning in the chapel, including Sunday. Then

you went to the eleven o'clock service at the church. A lot of guests went to church who didn't usually go; I think they thought my father would be rather shocked if they didn't go, so they went. In the church, not one sound of what was going on could be heard, because we sat in a chapel where, if you knew your prayer book and you'd lived there a long time, you knew more or less where you were, but many an Amen I've heard at the wrong moment.

Victoria Dane was brought up a Scottish Episcopal, but

we always went to the kirk on the first Sunday of the month because my father said as we were living in Scotland we must go. We didn't play

MAMMA: "To-morrow's Christmas Day, Effie, dear, and you will go to church for the first time." (Encouragingly): "There will be beautiful music——" Effie: "Oh, mummy, dear, may I dance?"

croquet on Sunday and I wasn't even allowed to take cards out to build a card house on Sunday. I was caught once, on the floor, building a card house – and the fuss! It was the most dreadful thing that ever happened. We weren't allowed to do a thing. We were allowed to go out on Sundays, supposedly for 'a quiet walk'. So we used to go cliff-climbing; nobody knew. There were terrific cliffs all around where we lived. But I was grown-up, married, with children, before we were ever allowed to play tennis on a Sunday. We had a beautiful grass tennis court. Once I said, 'Well, Mother, what can it matter? Really, it's ridiculous; I'm marking the lawn,' and she said, 'My dear, what would the servants say?' And of course the thing was, when I became independent I became rather anti-church.

'WE WENT TO CHURCH EVERY SUNDAY'

SPELDHURST CHURCH, 1906

The London child could not escape to the cliffs or disappear for the day in a donkey cart, but London had its compensations. 'The thing we always loved, of course, was the straw, or sometimes peat, which was put down in the streets if anybody was ill, to muffle the noise of wheels on the cobbles.'

London was full of noises, and each had its interest.

There was the last surviving street cry: 'Will you buy my sweet lavender? Three bunches for one penny?' You used to hear women singing that, quite commonly.

And there was the milkman:

he had a large brass churn and a lot of cans, which held a pint, or half a pint. He called 'Milko!' and that produced the kitchenmaid, who came running up the steps of the area with a jug. And the milkman's pony would stop, until the milkman called to him and he would then move on to the next area gate – he always knew exactly where to stop.

The muffin man

had his muffins on his head, on a wooden tray; he called 'Muffins and crumpets!' There were knife-grinders, boot blacks, street vendors of

PICCADILLY CIRCUS IN 1912

everything from matchboxes to little red, white and blue windmills, and the man who caned the chairs; he called 'Chair baskets to mend!'; the scrap merchant with his 'Any old iron!' and the newsboys shouting.

There was a constant noise of horses shaking their harness, from the mews behind the house; they often had bells in their harness, and you could hear the grooms hissing as they groomed the horses.

Carriages and vans rattled past, the note of the wheels changing as they came to the stones of the crossing, where the crossing sweeper waited:

There was a lot of dust and mud, dust in summer and mud in winter, and every so often, at the end of the street, there was a stone crossing kept free of mud by the crossing sweeper. I think the gentry were expected to give him a penny as they used his crossing.

Day and night there was the sound of whistling for cabs:

We had a whistle with a pea in it, kept in the hall. You opened the door and whistled; one whistle for a taxi, two for a hansom and three for a four-wheeler; your butler would blow the whistle at intervals and eventually a cab would turn up – that was the way they were summoned. Whistling for

MATCH SELLER

WON'T YOU BUY MY PRETTY
FLOWERS?

cabs was forbidden in the First War, because there were so many wounded soldiers and it disturbed them. So there was a decree that there should be no whistling; it never came back, after the war.

London smelt of the horses, which were everywhere. There were the horse-drawn buses, topless, 'with covers to put over your knees to keep off the rain; the rest of you just got wet. I remember making my wretched governess wait for a horse bus in Sloane Street, because they were getting rather rare.' Straining horses hauled the heavy wagons up the hill of Piccadilly,

which is quite considerable, so Our Dumb Friends League kept two or three trace horses at Hyde Park Corner. These were hitched to the wagons to help them up the hill and then they were unhitched and brought back. It must have been rather a dreary business for those horses; they were always pulling uphill. Men were employed to sweep the dung from the streets. We used to say they were very disgusting, because we thought they were sweeping it up with their hands. But it was pointed out that they had little shovels.

These sweepers often wore 'the very picturesque uniform of the employees of the Westminster Corporation – a slouch hat, turned up on the lefthand side, a rather splendid blue coat, and heavy boots.'

The cow at Storeys Gate, with her dairymaid, who would milk her into a glass to sell to passers-by, had gone, but there were still sheep in Green Park 'and very black they were'. Indeed all London was black:

KEEPING LONDON CLEAN

Every time you went out you had to change your gloves, and how the grown-ups managed with their long skirts I do not know. Of course, when my mother went out the footman would always put down a carpet to the car. It was kept in the hall and it would roly-poly out.

Our house looked out onto a wretched little half-moon, which we called the Grubby Gardens. That was my picture of the Garden of Eden. When God was walking in the cool of the evening, I pictured him as walking in the Grubby Gardens with Adam and Eve lurking behind the very sparse vegetation.

There were people constantly sweeping the streets and water carts were always going about, watering the roads to lay the dust, but of course nothing could clean the air. 'You couldn't possibly sit on the grass in the park, or lean against a railing, because you would have to change all your clothes.' The apotheosis of all this blackness was 'the pea-soup fog. Really frightening. That was an extraordinary thing in winter, the frequency of the real fogs, which are a thing completely of the past.'

It was a prodigious, bustling, wealthy, imperial, grimy city and yet it had an intimacy and cohesion, now destroyed. 'London is so

'STREET GROUP', ABOUT 1910

much bigger now, and so much more cut into bits.' Belgravia, for example, was a place where anybody could live because 'there were the palaces in Belgrave Square and the smaller houses in the streets off the square. . . .'

Wilton Crescent sounds immensely grand now, but then it just backed on to Belgrave Square, which was smart and expensive, but Wilton Crescent was quite an ordinary place to live for a man like my father, who was making his way at the Bar.

Behind the street there would be the mews 'with everything; the chemist, the carpenter, the window cleaner – the lot. It was a complete village and we knew them all.' There was also Kinnerton Street, winding its slummy way along the back of Wilton Place, and which was 'thought to be rough and we weren't allowed to go into it very much'. There were 'lots of little shops, chemists and bun-shops and so on – there wasn't this idea that everything had to be residential in certain areas.'

The heartland of Edwardian London was small. Kensington, for example, 'was thought rather dim', and one Edwardian lady remarked in horror, 'My dear, she's gone to live in SW1!' But small though it was, it was not the exclusive preserve of the very rich.

THE LAW

Chapter Three
LEARNING

THE GOVERNESS AND HER CHARGES

'EXIT TYRANNUS': THE GOVERNESS WEEPING ON THE DAY SHE LEAVES
(MAXFIELD PARRISH'S ILLUSTRATION FOR KENNETH GRAHAME'S
THE GOLDEN AGE)

In many houses, education is certainly not the highest expense. The cook is frequently paid at a higher rate than the governess. It is common for a governess to receive £30 to £60 a year and less, and it is also quite common for a cook's wages to be from £60 to £100 a year and more. (Arthur Ponsonby, *The Decline of Aristocracy*, 1912)

U ntil the age of eight, boys and girls did their lessons together in the schoolroom with a governess, or in London they might go to a 'little class': 'That was what people did: parents would club together and employ a teacher. Ours was very good, I think; she taught us to read and write, and numbers.' Then there was the dancing class, where you learned the waltz, the two-step polka, the Lancers, Sir Roger de Coverley and the Irish jig. 'We regarded it as perfectly dreadful and we were very uncooperative, I'm afraid, in the dancing class.' Slightly more amusing was the gym class in Alexandra Mansions, behind the Albert Hall, where the more proficient children climbed ropes and vaulted, while the little

'A LITTLE CLASS'

ones went upstairs and marched round to the music of a gramophone with a long horn, like the one through which the dog listened to His Master's Voice. 'But the teacher always put a duster in the horn to damp down the sound and we thought that rather a pity.'

In the country there was no little class; there had to be a governess for the girls, and the boys under eight. Governesses, ill paid and socially somewhat despised, were a mixed bag:

My governess was *not* very good. No, I was uneducated, myself. My sister learned to speak French and German very well and that was considered the right thing to do; I don't think people bothered much about education for girls; they got what they could get.

Leila Hampden's governess was a parson's daughter, 'a great scarecrow of a woman', found by an aunt. Her education was

a lovely feast of Rudyard Kipling and G. A. Henty but very little else. We learned by heart lengthy passages from the Bible, all carefully chosen, some warlike speeches from *Henry V* and the county capitals of Britain and the rivers they were on, the rudiments of English history, and arithmetic, out of the loathsome *Longman's Simple Arithmetic*. I was excluded from Latin but allowed instead to colour various maps of the world, enjoyable and satisfactory, with all the red for British possessions.

In remote parts of the country it was difficult to find and keep even a reasonably good governess:

THE GOVERNESS, AS SEEN BY *PUNCH*

Mamma. "Now go and say Good-night to your Governess, like a good little girl, and give her a Kiss."
Little Puss. "I'll say Good-night, but I won't give her a Kiss."
Mamma. "That's naughty! Why won't you give her a Kiss?"
Little Puss. "Because she slaps people's Faces when they try to Kiss her."
Mamma. "Now, don't talk Nonsense; but do as you're told."
Little Puss. "Well, Mummy, if you don't believe Me,——ask Papa!"

[*Tableau.*

My eldest brother and I got through, I can never remember whether it was ten governesses in thirteen years, or thirteen governesses in ten years – I think it was thirteen governesses. Either we hated them so much that my mother thought they must be cruel and she got rid of them, or she couldn't stand them, or Nanny couldn't stand them, or the governesses couldn't stand us. They literally just came and went. So my brothers went to school and I was left high and dry. I went to school when I was ten because the governesses wouldn't stay, and because it was very lonely, too, just me and one governess.

It must have been a bleak existence for the governess, uncomfortably placed between the servants and the family:

I don't quite know what my mother did about the governess in London – it sounds rather snob – but I don't suppose she would have really very much liked to put a French governess next to a guest, perhaps we were at a second table.

Surprisingly, there were some good governesses, such as Madeleine Vurpillot:

Capi, as we all called her, though very young was no means inexperienced. She had a good university degree and had taught both in Germany and America. She was a splendid person; she made me work hard and play hard. I did all my lessons in French, and we spoke it, both in and out of the schoolroom. During my three years with her, we had read the best of Molière, Racine and Corneille, and a lot of French lyrical poetry, and I was well grounded in French history. She was most exacting about one's accent; I had to practise my vowels every morning in front of my looking glass. In the summer we played tennis, and a kind of squash against a brick wall for between seasons. Bicycles played a big part in our lives. . . .

'BICYCLES PLAYED A BIG PART IN OUR LIVES'

Once Capi had taken over I was very nearly glad to start term, she was so alive, utterly different from anyone who had ever instructed me before.

Another enterprising governess was engaged by General Allenby for his son. Fired by Baden-Powell's book *Aid to Scouting*, she climbed a tree with her charge and successfully ambushed her employer. More typical, probably, was the dreary governess in a 1904 *Child's Own Magazine:*

Miss Morton grew quite cross, and told him to write out that four times four made sixteen, and that Dublin was on the Liffey, six times. At last he was finished. Miss Morton put on her hat and went off on her bicycle, spinning away along the white high road in a little cloud of dust.

ROYAL BICYCLISTS: PRINCESS MARY AND PRINCE HENRY

SCHOOLGIRL CROCODILE

Some girls went to boarding schools, either because they lived in remote places where governesses were hard to come by, or because their parents were overseas, but it was very unusual for upper-class girls to go to school. Lady Remnant and her sister went to a boarding school in Bexhill because her father was serving in India:

From the time I was eight or nine until I was about twelve I didn't see my parents at all; my father I didn't see until I was about fourteen, and then it was only for a short visit and I didn't see him again until I was eighteen. The normal child, with a home and a Nanny, would not, most probably, have gone to boarding school, and I think we led a much more grown-up life than most of our contemporaries, who were kept in the nursery and the schoolroom.

It was considered exciting and glamorous to go away to school instead of being stuck in the country with a governess, with

PORTRAIT OF A COUNTRY GIRL, 1904

perhaps only one or two girls of the right age living near, who were asked to tea occasionally. ('They were supposed to be our friends. How we loathed them.') 'At school we played hockey and cricket and tennis, and had a lovely time. I was very lucky with my friends at school; I used to go and stay with them all over the place, so I had a marvellous time in the holidays.'

The French Mademoiselle was a great feature:

My word, she got French into us! We had French-speaking tables at meals, and every day you had to go up to one of the two Mademoiselles and

'AT SCHOOL WE PLAYED ... CRICKET
AND TENNIS'

COOKERY CLASS, 1910

A SEWING CLASS

speak to her in French for five minutes – not about the weather! If they were in a good mood it was plain sailing, but if they were in a horrid mood they bit your head off. I can't remember ever being embarrassed about speaking French; it's a civilized language, why not speak it?

At school there were examinations to be faced: 'They were called the Oxford (or Cambridge) Junior and Senior. Those were the exams you took; there was no School Certificate.' When Lady Remnant was doing the Senior

quite suddenly they made it compulsory to do maths – geometry and algebra. That was an awful shock because we had never done either, and we had to get down to it and concentrate on geometry and algebra. The school imported a marvellous man to teach us. I never thought of going to university. I didn't know anyone at all who went to Oxford or Cambridge in those days. Not one of my friends went, not one. It's funny when you think of it now, but I never remember meeting a girl who was an under-graduate.

There were about thirty girls at Judith Lyttelton's school:

One girl wanted to go to Oxford, which caused great despondency because she was terribly special and had to have tutoring and everything else, and that was an event because no one had ever thought of wishing to go to Oxford. I quite wanted to go, but my mother said no. 'Who would you meet at Oxford? Would there be anybody you would like?' That was the sort of attitude. You wouldn't have anything in common with the other girls.

Grizel Hartley's mother wanted her to go to Girton

because she had had two friends who were early Girtons, the Miss Durhams. But she was very anxious that I shouldn't be highbrow, because of my aunts, who were. She thought they were rather stuck all over with safety pins and didn't have enough baths – which I think they probably were. And so she was rather ambivalent about it.

BOTANY CLASS AT A LONDON SCHOOL FOR GIRLS, 1908

'A certain sort of education is provided for girls which places them sometimes on a higher intellectual level than their brothers,' wrote Arthur Ponsonby. Perhaps he was thinking of such schools as Cheltenham Ladies' College, which was thought to be highly intellectual and was attended by some girls almost by accident, because Cheltenham was a place where soldier fathers tended to live when they left the army. Grizel Hartley, who lived in Hammersmith, went to St Paul's Girls' School every day in a tram, attended by a maid; 'other people didn't have maids. She was very nice but I used to try to get rid of her as soon as I could.' St Paul's had only recently been built, by the Mercers' Company

who must have been very rich in those days, and everything was very well done – the organ was marvellous, the chairs were marvellous, the desks were marvellous, and it was very large and alarming.

PROCTOR AND BULLDOGS, CAMBRIDGE

'GET YOU TO GIRTON, BEATRICE; GET YOU TO NEWNHAM: HERE'S NO PLACE FOR YOU MAIDS.' WOMEN'S DEGREES, CAMBRIDGE, 1897

The headmistress was Miss Gray; she was the founding head and she stayed for a long time, until about 1926 or 1927. She was Irish; very, very imposing, very alarming. She had grey hair so we naturally thought she was old, but I suppose she can't have been more than forty or so when I was there. There were some excellent teachers – not all were good, by any means, but we had a wonderful history mistress, and for classics we had Miss Postgate, who realized that the important thing was not to translate every word correctly. She used to read us bits of Catullus and tried to explain to us the point of it all; she was very good that way. It wasn't difficult to get into any university from St Paul's, not in the least. I wanted to be a vet, and I did my first medical from there. I think I was the first person to do it from the school. When I went up to Cambridge I didn't have to do any work for the first year – by which time I'd lost the habit. But I had a lovely time.

The music master at St Paul's was the composer Gustav Holst:

He lived in the school, more or less. He wasn't at all celebrated or well known then, and he had a wife and child and not much money. He wasn't very good at keeping order, and he wasn't very good at teaching (he taught singing, and the organ), but everyone loved him; he was awfully nice. The best part was that all the schoolrooms opened onto the big hall, and all the time he wasn't teaching, he was there, playing the organ, mostly Bach. That's how I know quite a lot of Bach. You could go and turn over for him, if you liked.

THE BOYS OF A CORNISH VILLAGE SCHOOL

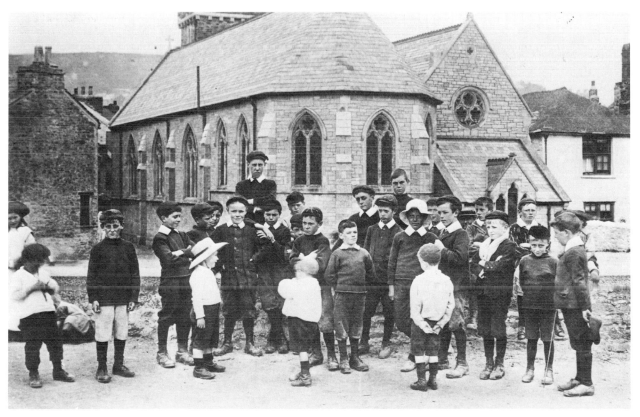

SPORTING HERO: W. G. GRACE AT THE NETS

'SCHOOL OUTFITS AND ALL ATHLETIC
REQUISITES'

WINCHESTER COLLEGE: THE VISIT OF
KING GEORGE V AND QUEEN MARY, 1912

Grizel Hartley went on to read biology at Cambridge, followed by philosophy at Lausanne. 'I can't say I learned much philosophy, but as it was of course all in French I did at least learn French.'

This was an education that the boys might have envied. They were dispatched to boarding schools at the age of eight, and the memory of homesickness is still vivid after seventy years:

The night before I went, I think I was rather excited; I remember there was a ball being given in one of the houses on the other side of the road and 'My Little Grey Home in the West' was the tune they were always playing. In the morning we set out to drive to Oxford. We got to Summerfields; I was rather excited, with the other new boys. But my mother spent the night in Oxford – perhaps it was rather a mistake – in order to come and see me the next day. I remember now, she said, 'Won't you be rather cold? Hadn't you better fetch your coat?' So I went to collect my coat, and the bell rang for the end of break – and I couldn't get back to her. And that absolutely finished me. However, I suppose it lasted about a week, of appalling misery, but after that it was all right. I arrived at Summerfields with a gold half sovereign, which was handed over to Mr Crofts, who kept it, and kept the stamps, and the sticking plaster, and the nibs – all the things which we had invested in. But in the end I had rather a splendid term, because I won all the prizes for every conceivable thing – Latin prose and so on.

'SPARE THE BRUSH AND SPOIL THE
TEETH': DENTAL HYGIENE CLASS

SCHOOL TEACHERS RECEIVING PUPILS'
PENNIES

Some boys never quite got used to going back to school:

It was that last home breakfast which did him in. He would come into the
dining room pale but dry-eyed, he turned his back to us to lift the lids off
the dishes, but when he came back to the table tears were always pouring
down his cheeks.

'The teaching at Winchester was abominable', according to one
Wykehamist. 'Latin wasn't so bad, but Greek!' The emphasis at
most schools was heavily on the business of 'character building'
which was supposed to produce men who were, in an unforgett-
able phrase, 'acceptable at a dance and invaluable in a shipwreck'.
It seems to have had some effect, for Baden-Powell remarked
proudly of his South African Constabulary, 'Nearly two thousand of
the men were public school men. With such a personnel it was
possible to put them on their honour and to trust them to do their
work in their scattered out-stations.' At Rugby, for example, the
boys got up at quarter to six, had a cold bath and then had a lesson
before they had breakfast. There was a roll-call three times a day.
The younger boys were kept on their toes, listening for the cry of
'Fag', which they rushed to answer because the last boy to arrive
had to do the job:

I fagged for a brute of a boy at Winchester. He would hide little pieces of paper to see if you dusted his room properly and you were beaten if you hadn't. I met him again years later, and he said, 'I suppose you'll be giving me lunch,' and I said, 'No, I shall certainly not give you lunch!' Most satisfying.

I once had a formal fight with another boy. We had seconds, rounds, the whole thing, and when we both had black eyes we shook hands and that was the end. It was just like *Tom Brown's Schooldays*.

Some of the houses at Winchester were better, but my house was terribly rough. I saw a lot of bullying. I remember a boy who was roasted in front of the fire. And there were endless beatings, by the boys, with an ash stick. But I only ever beat two boys. They were throwing bottles and they insulted the poor old matron – they were terrible bullies. So I gave them a good hiding and I never had any trouble after that. I'd done it once, and they knew I could do it, so that was the end. I'd seen too much bullying. But I wasn't unhappy. You were beaten and that was the end of it. Anyway, I was always off fishing, or shooting. Fishing was by invitation, on the Test, and I had a friend with a gun which he carried in a rolled-up umbrella and we'd come back with a brace of pheasants which were cooked for us.

The teaching at most public schools was somewhat single-minded, specializing in classics. Maurice Bowra recalled in his memoirs that:

the classical side at Cheltenham was devised to win scholarships at Oxford and Cambridge. . . . The means designed to reach this end had serious drawbacks. For our last three years we specialized in classics and almost nothing else except some scripture, which amounted to classics since it consisted of a study of St Paul in Greek, and a weekly essay, which was necessary since it was demanded in the scholarship examinations.

Relaxation at Cheltenham consisted of games and the occasional lantern-slide show; 'there was no art, no handicraft, no music, no acting, no dancing with the girls from the Ladies' College.'

'There *were* mathematicians at Winchester,' recalls my father, 'but they weren't thought much of. Nearly all the clever boys did classics.' The heroes, at most schools, were the athletes. Rupert Brooke when at Rugby wrote 'A Child's Guide to Rugby School' for the school magazine in which he advised the new boys, who arrived having 'read a lot of Henty, the headlines of the *Daily Mail* and first-class cricket averages', that they should pay attention to the athlete. 'Regard all such with immense reverence and awe; it is for them that all Public schools are founded and conducted. And they know it.' Sure enough, Brooke himself, winner of the school poetry prize and a classical scholarship to King's, was summed up in the Rugby school magazine as follows:

R. C. Brooke weighs 11 stone 12 pounds and is a reliable centre three-quarter who, though not brilliant, is usually in his place and makes good openings; he tackles too low.

Chapter Four
READING

UGANDA: MISSIONARY FLEEING FROM
LIONS, *BOY'S OWN PAPER*

THE CORAL ISLAND

R·M·BALLANTYNE

BALLANTYNE'S *THE CORAL ISLAND*

'You jolly well let that alone,' exclaimed Bunter warmly. 'I haven't finished reading it yet. I say, you fellows, it's a jolly good story – all about a boarding school for burglars, with the headmaster a crook, and the assistant masters all convicts. A true-life story, you know. . . .'

'We loved our books and we read them over and over again. We had no libraries you see, school libraries or public libraries, so our books were very important to us.'

Many of the books which appeared for Edwardian Christmases and birthdays are still on children's shelves today: Beatrix Potter, *Little Black Sambo*, Rudyard Kipling, *Peter Pan*, *The Wind in the Willows* and E. Nesbit. There were also the older favourites: *Alice in Wonderland*, *The Water Babies*, *Treasure Island*, *Tom Brown's Schooldays*, *Black Beauty*, Hans Andersen and *Grimms' Fairy Tales*. All these are timeless in their appeal; it is the less distinguished writing for children which holds a clearer mirror to the world of an Edwardian child.

"Three years ago we started taking your magazine, since when we have been nowhere without it."

The Children's Encyclopædia, the only book in the world which has ever been turned into a monthly magazine, is reaching its third birthday in its new form. Take it home with Popular Science. No children's journal ever issued has won so many grown-up friends as the

CHILDREN'S MAGAZINE

which goes, on the 15th of every month, into over forty countries, and can be bought for sevenpence on any bookstall. Be sure you get the Little Paper, the only newspaper written for boys and girls.

Children's Magazine   They are only
and the Little Paper   Sevenpence

'WE READ THEM OVER AND OVER AGAIN'

'There was great emphasis on "improving books". I had a phase of reading *Answers* which was absolutely forbidden. I can remember now going round to the head gardener's wife because she had it. I simply can't think what was wrong with *Answers*, perhaps it was just not improving.'

Answers, launched in the eighties, was a popular journal, not aimed at children in particular, on which were founded the fortunes of Alfred Harmsworth, later Lord Northcliffe, and his Amalgamated Press. Parents did their best to introduce their offspring to a better class of literature.

'My father was a tremendous reader and used to read aloud to us a lot, which is how I know Shakespeare and a great deal of Scott, which we loved.' Scott seems to have been a general favourite at this period. 'We were all Scottites,' said Judith Lyttelton, while Lady Remnant remembers that:

My sister and I always used to have our tea on our own, in a small sitting room which was handed over to us, and my sister read, always; she tilted her chair back and she read, all through tea, the Waverley novels. I adored her, but I used to get very bored with all the reading.

Secure in their nurseries and schoolrooms, children had an insatiable appetite for adventure and deeds of daring, and their stomachs were strong. After all, many of them had been reared on Struwwelpeter, 'which no psychiatrist now will allow anywhere near a child, but the effect was extremely bracing'. Hoffman created Struwwelpeter in the 1840s to amuse his son. He intended it to be a comical parody of contemporary moral tales but later children took it quite seriously and shuddered at the Great Big Scissor Man who cut off Conrad's thumbs ('Ah!' said Mamma, 'I knew he'd come/To naughty little Suck-a-Thumb') and at the fate of poor Harriet, who played with matches and was burnt alive.

Children then graduated to such books as *The Coral Island*. The following is one among many of Ballantyne's gory passages:

As we reached the verge of the wood, we discovered the savages surrounding the large war-canoe, which they were apparently on the point of launching. Suddenly the multitude put their united strength to the canoe; but scarcely had the huge machine begun to move, when a yell, the most appalling that ever fell upon my ear, rose high above the shouting of the

STRUWWELPETER

BEAR-HUG, 1904

savages. It had not died away when another and another smote upon my throbbing ear; and then I saw that these inhuman monsters were actually launching their canoe over the living bodies of their victims. But there was no pity in the breasts of these men. Forward they went in ruthless indifference, shouting as they went, while high above their voices rang the dying shrieks of these wretched creatures, as, one after another, the ponderous canoe passed over them, burst the eyeballs from their sockets, and sent the life blood gushing from their mouths. O reader, this is no fiction. I would not, for the sake of thrilling you with horror, invent so terrible a scene. It was witnessed. It is true – true as that accursed sin which has rendered the human heart capable of such diabolical enormities!

TYPICAL *BOP* COVER

ADVERTISEMENTS IN THE *BOY'S OWN PAPER*

It is strange after this to turn back to Ballantyne's preface and read that 'if there is any boy or man who loves to be melancholy and morose, and who cannot enter into the regions of fun, let me seriously advise him to shut my book and put it away. It is not meant for him. . . .'

Fenimore Cooper, another favourite, was little better, and as for the boys' magazines, no modern parent would have them in the house. The Aldine Company, for example, started its *New Buffalo Bill Library* in 1899 with the claim that it would not shock 'the most fastidious' and with the first instalment of a serial in which the heroine receives her lover's scalp and eyeballs wrapped up in a parcel.

Scalping was frequent in tales of the Wild West but happily some victims survived their ghastly fate. In a *Boys' Herald* of 1903, Dan the trapper

snatched off his square skin cap, making the boy spring to his feet aghast with horror, while the dog started back glaring at the visitor and bursting forth into a deep angry bay.

'Horrible!' came from Wat Waring's lips, – one word only but meaning so much, for the sight he gazed upon was terrible indeed, his visitor standing transformed into a hideous object as with one quick motion he laid bare the trace of a frightful act of triumph of the savage redskin over his defeated enemy, the trapper's head, with its long-healed scars looking strangely white above his sun-bronzed face, telling the tale, in its frightful bareness, of the rapid placing round of the savage's knife and the tearing away of the scalp.

In 1910 the veteran *Boy's Own Paper* proudly published some of its testimonials: ' "Will delight the heart of any healthy-minded schoolboy" – *Practical Teacher.* "The boy must be hard to please who is not satisfied with the *Boy's Own Paper*" – English Churchman.'

It was read by girls as well as boys, and, judging by some of the advertisements in its pages, by adults as well. True, there were the offers of 'Valuable Stamps Free', 'Handwriting Taught By Post', 'How To See Halley's Comet – Special Offer of a Powerful Solar and Terrestial Telescope fitted with Achromatic-Combination Lenses' with 'Free, to each Purchaser, a Unique Working Model size 12 inches by 10 inches – prepared at considerable expense by E. Rupert Hicks, Esq., FRAS – showing the positions assumed by Halley's Comet in relation to the Earth and Sun', all for 10s. 6d. Even 'Indian Parrot and cage; 6s. or offer; also pigskin leggings, 3s.' might be expected to appeal to boys. But what about 'Smokers' Tooth-powders (perfumed) 1s. 3d. Immediate delivery' and 'Old Artificial Teeth Bought, any condition. 4d. vulcanite, 9d. on silver, 1s. 3d. on gold, 2s. 6d. on platinum'?

The *Boy's Own Paper* was approved by parents because it was instructive and could be relied upon to maintain a high moral tone. The editor adopted an authoritarian line with his correspondents. Here is his answer to 'An Unhappy Reader': 'Really there is nothing to worry about, and as you grow older you will find many more in the same position. The best thing to do is to keep the knowledge to yourself, as it is of no interest to anybody else.' He was equally forthright with G. H. Leakey: 'You should join the Canadian Navy, the posters about which are on every hoarding in Canada. The idea of coming all the way from Alberta on the chance of joining the Royal Navy is not to be encouraged'; and tart with J. Parker: 'If you

'NOBLESSE OBLIGE'

had read the correspondence column, you would know that the invariable answer is – get *The Sea*, published by the Shipping Gazette, New Street Square, EC.'

The articles stressed the merits of manliness and an open-air life: 'few men could stand the strain, either mentally or physically, but the Bempton egg-gatherers are men of iron nerve and muscles powerful as steel bars.' Even an article on Westminster was headed 'Athletes in Parliament' and begins:

Looking through the list of Members of Parliament after the recent General Election, one is struck by the large number of men who have given evidence of their prowess in some form of sport, and without a doubt their athletic training will stand them in good stead during the strenuous life of a Member of the House of Commons. . . . It would be an easy matter to form a splendid Parliamentary eleven from the men who have been known to fame as cricketers.

'SOME HUMOURS OF THE WHEEL'
(FROM THE *BOY'S OWN PAPER*)

'THREE MINUTES TO "LOCK UP" AND ONE MILE TO GO!'

Readers could identify with 'A Trooper of Constabulary': ' "Come, come," said the Colonel, "cheer up, my boy. We'll soon make a soldier of you. You are the kind of man we want over there at the Cape." ' . . . How my mother's knitting needles flew while warm socks and woollen cholera belts seemed to grow like magic under her nimble fingers!' The boys were encouraged to collect war medals, particularly those from South Africa and Rhodesia – 'The design is soul-stirring; it is the British Lion charging, with tail erect, although wounded by an assegai.'

Although much mellowed from the vintage blood and thunder of the late nineteenth century, *BOP* still contained some strong stuff. In 1912 the hero of a serial called 'Jeffrey of the White Wolf Trail' found himself in a tight spot at the mercy of a gang of villains, one of whom remarks:

'There is nothing like a red-hot ramrod for making tongues wag. Placed near the eyes it is a wonderful persuader and when it insinuates its way into the flesh it can make the dumb speak.'

Nicholls took the white-hot ramrod, twirled it once or twice in the air and then laid it deliberately on the top of Jack's ear. For a moment the unfortunate sufferer did not realize the anguish, but as the hot metal burnt his ear and singed his head the intolerable smarting made him scream out with a pitiful intensity. The smell of burning flesh became apparent.

Of course the gang soon came to a sticky end at the hands of the Sioux:

The white men were simply hacked to pieces by the heavy blows of the Indian tomahawks and so terrible was the massacre that not even a fragment of scalp could be secured by the triumphant braves.

The school and scouting stories, though milder in tone, were equally strong on morals ('Fox Junior, aetat. 10, was a little sneak . . .') and solidly middle class in vocabulary ('honour bright', 'playing fair', 'beastly good of you').

'The books we had were all very moral, but the odd thing is that we never noticed it.' Schoolboy heroes were always frank and manly and almost invariably suspected of some underhand deed, but in the end they always triumphed over the slackers, rotters, blackguards and cads. The stories had titles like 'Schoolboy Grit', 'King of Ranleigh' or, more pretentiously, 'Noblesse Oblige', even 'Veritas Prevalebit'. Some were straightforward tales of school life, others were adventure stories in a school setting, for it was, wrote E. S. Turner

'THE BOOKS WE HAD WERE ALL VERY MORAL'

that agreeable period when steam men puffed across the prairie trampling Indians underfoot; when the elect of Britain's boarding schools set off every other week by balloon or submarine to discover a lost city or a vanishing island; when almost every Northcliffe boys' paper carried a serial describing the invasion of Britain by Germans, French or Russians; when well-nigh every tramp, ice-cream vendor, organ grinder or muffin man turned out to be Sexton Blake; and when every self-respecting football team had its mysterious masked centre-forward.

In these circumstances the plain school story seemed rather tame.

R. S. Warren Bell's *The Mystery of Markham* had all the classic ingredients. In the words of a contemporary review:

The scene of this captivating school tale is called Tarport College, but every boy who is lucky enough to read the book will soon find himself substituting his own college for Tarport; with such faithful cunning and broad realism does the author line in the school atmosphere and the schoolboy types. The keen joys and rivalries of 'footer' and cricket, and the annual sports, are set down here in glowing terms, and he must be a strangely-built young person whose blood does not run the quicker for following the fortunes of Tarport, in the field of sport. A boy with a mystery about him is pretty certain to be an unpopular boy, and Markham has the misfortune to be regarded as 'mysterious' by his fellows. A fine sportsman and one that Tarport can ill afford to spare, Markham nevertheless declines to play regularly for the school and gives no adequate reason for his frequent conspicuous absence.

LITTLE FOLKS ANNUAL

READING ARTHUR MEE'S *LITTLE PAPER*

This behaviour, which would scarcely raise an eyebrow today, had a compelling explanation: 'Markham's mother is forced to keep a boarding-house owing to straitened circumstances.' The excitement came in with

the strange boarders in her establishment, who include among their number a member of the Secret Service and the proprietor of a picture-theatre. The sequel involves the arrest of a foreign spy, and is made all the more thrilling by the tunnelling operations of the amusing family that live next door to Markham.

The reader of such stories was left in no doubt as to where his sympathies should lie; it was a bad mark to be uninterested in games. Here is a typical villain:

Sinclair was about as unpopular in the school as Roy was the reverse. Why, no one quite knew, excepting for the fact that he did not care for games and yet made no attempt to shine in his school work, and was usually put down as a 'rotter'. He had no chum and not many casual friends. He was a tall, lanky boy with straw-coloured hair and no eyelashes worth mentioning, while his eyes were of the kind usually termed 'shifty'.

Naturally, when the hero was accused of destroying the portrait of Mr Hilton's wife, who had recently died 'with tragic suddenness', anyone, except Roy's friends, could see that Sinclair must be responsible. Even Mr Hilton was not deceived by the weight of evidence against Roy:

Mr Hilton looked at him keenly as he put the books down, then suddenly spoke. 'Wait a minute, Tremaine; I want to speak to you, my boy.'

Tremaine waited sullenly, for he thought Mr Hilton was about to advise him to confess, and he was getting tired of that piece of counsel.

But the master had no intention of doing anything of the kind. Quietly putting his hand on the boy's shoulder, he said, 'Tremaine, I do not believe you spoiled my picture.'

Roy could hardly believe his ears. 'You don't believe it, sir? I thought everybody believed it. Nearly all my friends do, so I don't see why you shouldn't.'

'Perhaps not, but I don't. You are a troublesome boy, but I don't believe you are a sneak or a cad.'

What other opinion could there be of 'a cheerful, lively and popular boy, with good abilities and a remarkable aptitude for all games'?

The contributors to boys' magazines included some fine writers, notably P. G. Wodehouse, and some of the stories became schoolboy classics. None were more popular than the annals of Greyfriars School and Billy Bunter (William George Bunter, of Bunter Court) which appeared in the *Magnet*. The comic genius of their author, Charles Hamilton (alias Frank Richards) cut across all barriers,

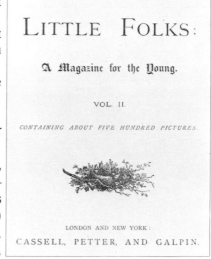

LITTLE FOLKS:

A Magazine for the Young.

VOL. II.

CONTAINING ABOUT FIVE HUNDRED PICTURES.

LONDON AND NEW YORK:

CASSELL, PETTER, AND GALPIN.

appealing to all classes and both sexes. In a typical incident the floundering Bunter is in trouble for playing tricks with a pin:

'No, sir! Nothing of the kind,' stuttered the confused Fat Owl. 'I never had a pin, sir. Besides, fellows are allowed to have pins, sir. I – I – I – was going to pin a page into my Latin grammar, sir. Not that I had a pin, sir!' added Bunter cautiously. 'You can ask Skinner, sir. He knows – he gave it to me.'

BILLY BUNTER

The Billy Bunter stories are still read and enjoyed and have even been printed in braille, but another immensely prolific and successful author, G. A. Henty, has not lasted so well. Henty wrote dashing adventure stories with titles like *With Clive in India*, *By Sheer Pluck*, *St George for England*, *The Dash for Khartoum*, *At the Point of the Bayonet* and *A Knight of the White Cross*. His life should have given him plenty of good material, for he had served in the Crimea before becoming a journalist, and was war correspondent for the *Standard* in the Austro-Italian war of 1866, the war in Abyssinia, the Franco-German War of 1870 and the Ashanti war of 1873–74.

It is sometimes said that there is no good to be obtained from tales of fighting and bloodshed. Believe it or not, War has its lessons as well as Peace. . . . The courage of our forefathers has created the greatest empire in the world around a small and in itself insignificant island. If this empire is ever lost, it will be by the cowardice of their descendants.

Henty never hesitated to break off a story in order to devote whole chapters to textbook history, thinly disguised as the words of some impossibly knowledgeable armourer or captain, and the writing was long-winded and stilted. E. Nesbit had a dig at historical novels of the Henty type in *The Treasure Seekers*, where the children take it in turns to write a serial story. Dora wrote the first chapter:

The sun was setting behind a romantic-looking tower when two strangers might have been observed descending the crest of the hill. The elder, a man in the prime of life; the other a handsome youth who reminded everybody of Quentin Durward. They approached the Castle in which the fair Lady Alicia awaited her deliverers. She leaned from the castellated window and waved her lily hand as they approached. They returned her signal, and retired to seek rest and refreshment at a neighbouring hostelry.

None the less Henty could always be relied upon to put in plenty of action – daring escapes, fights against terrible odds – and he is remembered with affection.

'Manliness' included blood sports, of course, and while it was very much frowned upon to be unkind to dogs, cats and horses, the slaughter of wild animals was quite another thing. Major-General E. Smith Brook, CB, wrote a series of articles for the *Boy's Own*

Paper on 'Some Experiences with Big Game', which read very oddly today. Here is the author hunting giraffe:

He gave me a rattling gallop of a mile and a half, during which time I put six bullets into him . . . he did not offer the slightest resistance – giraffes never do. . . . I cut off his tail as a trophy and left him.

Rhinoceros we hunted in the same way as the elephants. Once we came up to them, they were easily killed with hardened bullets, and we shot a great many. They are, without exception, the ugliest of animals, and they are very savage when wounded. They are also plucky brutes.

Similar attitudes appear in a children's board game called *Whaling*, in which 'the fact that the whales progress around the board and occasionally disappear adds considerably to the amusement'; each player was a 'whaler' and moved a cardboard boat around the board, harpooning whales as he went. Evidently this was before the days of conservation. Consider the article 'The Story of a Fur Coat' in Arthur Mee's *Children's Encyclopaedia*, in which a beautiful lady, wearing 'an ulster of costly furs', comes to visit a sick child and ends by instructing her about the fur trade.

'You are resting your little cheek, here in London, against the fur of an animal that once ranged a desolate country far beyond any trace of humanity. If this animal had not lived there, that country would have remained desolate to this day. . . . If women in London were content with sheep-skins instead of fur coats, there would now be a vast quarter of the globe untrodden by the foot of man, thousands of people out of work, and hundreds of cities unbuilt . . .'

'And this beautiful soft coat,' said Emmy, stroking the garment, 'once upon a time had a great beast inside it; and now it has got an angel!'

At the same period, a counterblast to the big game hunter came from the works of the Canadian author Ernest Thompson Seton. Illustrated by hundreds of his drawings of animals in the wild, these books, *Wild Animals I Have Known*, *Lives of the Hunted*, *The Biography of a Grizzly*, *The Biography of a Silver Fox* and the rest, were 'derived from close and loving observation of nature, careful not to humanize their subjects, seeking to get inside the skins of wild creatures and understand their motives and emotions', as a contemporary review put it. As Seton wrote in *The Biography of a Silver Fox*:

I had been a fox-hunter myself and had learned to love a foxhound, but the sight of the splendid creature that day, pursued by a very hellhound, remorseless, tireless, inevadable, gave me the feeling as of seeing some beautiful bird of song being crushed by a poisonous reptile. The traditional league of man and dog was then and there forgot. Thenceforth my heart was all with the Silver Fox.

Girls came off worse than boys when it came to children's fiction. E. Nesbit parodied 'The books they give you for a prize at a girls school – I mean a ''Young Ladies'' school, of course – not a high school. High schools are not nearly so silly as some other kinds.'

'Ah, me' sighed a slender maiden of twelve summers, removing her elegant hat and passing her tapery finger lightly through her fair tresses, 'How sad it is – is it not? – to see able-bodied youths and young ladies wasting the precious summer hours in idleness and luxury.'

The maiden frowned reproachingly, but yet with earnest gentleness, at the group of youths and maidens who sat beneath the umbragipeaous beech tree and ate blackcurrants.

'Dear brothers and sisters,' the blushing girl went on, 'could we not, even now, at the eleventh hour, turn to account these wasted lives of ours, and seek some occupation at once improving and agreeable?'...

'It's no use. I can't write like these books. I wonder how the books' authors can keep it up.'

What really happened was that we were all eating blackcurrants in the orchard, out of a cabbage leaf, and Alice said –

'I say, look here, let's do something. It's simply silly to waste a day like this. It's just on eleven. Come on!' (*The Wouldbegoods*, 1901)

The *Girl's Own Paper*, from the same stable as the *Boy's Own Paper*, is a mine of stories of the kind E. Nesbit was parodying, either romantic and earnest, or romantic and humorous, with such unpromising titles as 'A Club of Fair Women', 'A Maiden of Dreams', 'Love or Lucre', 'The Discipline of Emmeline Hope'. 'Barty's Love Story' boasted a heroine with 'young life, flowing as a fountain with lillied romance and reflecting so clearly the soul's exquisite star', while the hero loved her with 'not an iota of sentimentality. His love was the overlord's love – powerful as Orion, tender as a violet's stalk, warm and white as the swan's breast.' The author of 'Rachel Fairlie, B A' set out to strike a blow for women's education and the hero was rather less heroic than some:

That old feeling of awe and reverence which had flooded her heart on the evening of the College social came full upon her now. 'Rachel,' he said impressively, 'we are pledged, you and I, to this mighty mission. Can you bear it? Are you strong enough, little girl?'...

A cry of distress burst from her lips. His face was deathly pale. His emotion had quite overpowered him, and utterly drained his strength. A curious faintness came over him. Staggering back, he fell heavily to the earth in a dead swoon.

THE *GIRL'S OWN PAPER*

WHEN MAN HAS CONQUERED THE AIR

There will, no doubt, be many improvements in flying machines once men have agreed that the aeroplanes are the best means of sailing in the air. The machines will, no doubt, be made smaller than at present, and all sorts of things will be done to enable them to carry as many passengers as possible, and to come easily to rest at stations. Large platforms will probably be erected as we see on the left of this picture, and beneath the airship long springs may be placed like those used on sledges, so that the great machines may fly up to their stations and drop slowly down on to the platform, where passengers will get out and descend to the ground by elevators.

GOP features ranged from the Fidelio Club (advice to amateur pianists) and the Palette Club (for artists) to moral guidance, household hints and how a girl should dress: 'I do set great faith in dark drills. I once had a poppy-coloured drill gown which did not require washing for three seasons.'

Readers who wrote to the magazine signed themselves 'Back-slider', 'A Stray Blossom', 'Looking Upward' and 'Lassie'; the editor's replies were effusive: 'Yours is a full and precious letter, dear.' 'No wonder you are depressed at times, poor darling.'

The correspondents seem to have been an odd lot, and even the editor's patience ran short at times:

Viti writes from Fiji to ask for two poems. One begins: 'They sat in silence side by side, He and she'. The second begins: 'Two maidens fair with pretty hair'. We are not struck by the poetical beauty of these extracts and should not have thought them worth tracing.

It must have been a relief to turn to the fat blue volumes of *The Children's Encyclopaedia*. This came out in 1908 and was a lucky dip of all kinds of information. The Skies at Night, Golden Deeds, Famous Books, Bible Stories, The Child's Book of Wonder, The Child's Book of Familiar Things, Egypt's Wonderful Story, fairy stories, poems and rhymes, Things to Make and Things to Do, all were jumbled together and, in spite of an unfortunate tendency to talk down to children (scales were called 'Fairy Ladders' and sharps and flats were 'little goblins'), *The Children's Encyclopaedia* went down well.

Another familiar sight was H. E. Marshall's *Our Island Story*: a child's history of England. 'That's really the only history I can now remember,' admitted one Edwardian. Simple verdicts, vivid stories, large and colourful pictures were Marshall's recipe for success:

Richard I was a good knight and a brave soldier, but he was not a good king... King John's heart was black and wicked.... Charles II was lazy selfish and deceitful, a bad man and a bad king. Yet Charles found both men and women to love him during his life and to sorrow for him at his death because he was clever, good-tempered and had pleasant manners.

There would certainly be a row of fairy stories on the Edwardian nursery shelf: the blood-curdling Grimm, Andrew Lang's many volumes of fairytales, and others, variable in quality. The Fairy Queen in Evelyn Sharp's *The Weathercock* 'was dressed in sunshine and roses. She wore a crown made of babies' smiles and rubies, and necklace made of babies' curls and diamonds.' If Edwardian children could stomach a good deal of blood and thunder, they could also tolerate quantities of saccharine. Mrs Molesworth was a prolific and successful purveyor of baby talk and fairies, but there were many more of the same kind:

> Mabel dreamt that out of her feet
> Two beautiful foxgloves grew
> And from out each flower fairies sweet
> Came seated on globes of dew

was an offering from *Mr Punch's Book for Children* of 1902.

Fairy stories were sentimental and bright; another popular vein was to be sentimental and gloomy. Deathbed scenes were common, and harrowing. Our family copy of *Misunderstood* has been wept over so often that the last pages, which describe the death of the poor, unloved, maligned little hero, have almost melted away. The most moving of them all was Mrs Ewing's *Jackanapes*, who risked and lost his life, riding back to save his friend on the battlefield:

'What about Jackanapes?'

'Don't you know? Sad business. Rode back for Johnson, and brought him in; but monstrous ill-luck, hit as they rode. Left lung – '

'Will he recover?'

'No. Sad business. What a frame – what limbs – what health – and what good looks! Finest young fellow – '

'Where is he?'

'In his own tent,' said the surgeon sadly.

The Major wheeled and left him. Later, Jackanapes asked the Major to say a prayer for him:

''Pon my soul I can only remember the little one at the end.'

'Please,' whispered Jackanapes.

Pressed by the conviction that what little he could do it was his duty to do, the Major – kneeling – bared his head, and spoke loudly, clearly and very reverently –

'The Grace of our Lord Jesus Christ – '

Jackanapes moved his left hand to his right one, which still held the Major's –

' – the love of GOD' and with that – Jackanapes died.

The queen of the deathbed scene was Charlotte M. Yonge; time, it seemed, could not wither her. *The Daisy Chain*, for example, was published in 1856 but was still being reprinted almost every year in the 1900s. The death of the saintly Margaret is only one of the deaths scattered through *The Daisy Chain*'s 600 pages:

MRS EWING'S *JACKANAPES*

It was midnight, on the longest night of the year; Ethel was lying on her bed, and had fallen into a brief slumber, when her father's low, clear voice summoned her: 'Ethel, she is going!'

There was a change on the face, and the breath came in labouring gasps. Richard lifted her head, and her eyes once more opened; she smiled once more.

'Papa!' she said, 'dear papa!'

He threw himself on his knees beside her, but she looked beyond him: 'Mamma! Alan! oh! there they are! More! more!' and, as though the unspeakable dawned on her, she gasped for utterance, then looked with a consoling smile on her father. 'Over now!' she said – and the last struggle was ended. That which Richard laid down was no longer Margaret May.

THE SAINTLY MARGARET, FROM CHARLOTTE M. YONGE'S *THE DAISY CHAIN*

Over now! The twenty-five years' life, the seven years' captivity on her couch, the anxious headship of the motherless household, the hopeless betrothal, the long suspense, the efforts for resignation, the widowed affections, the slow decay, the tardy, painful death agony – all was over; nothing left save what they had rendered the undying spirit, and the impress her example had left on those around her.

Patriotism was another favourite theme. Mary Clive wrote:

We assumed that patriotism was one of the basic virtues, like courage, truth or unselfishness. There has been so much debunking in the last fifty years that it is an effort to remember how delightfully simple world affairs

MRS HODGSON BURNETT, WHO WROTE
LITTLE LORD FAUNTLEROY AND *THE
SECRET GARDEN*

used to look – the whites so white and the blacks so black, and England always in the right.

This was exactly the note so frequently sounded by Edwardian children's authors. Herbert Strang's *Sultan Jim: Empire Builder* is a good example.

Very few of Mr Strang's readers, it is safe to say, will close the book until they have followed Jim's career to its triumphant consummation when, after many tough fights with cannibals, he at length, like some modern Moses, leads a down-trodden and peculiar tribe out of the wilderness of danger into a promised land of protection beneath the British flag.

Pictorial Comedy.

1. *M. Le Poyntes:* "Ah, ze balmy air of ze fine weather in ze park I vill sit and enjoy!"

2. *The Nurse:* "Now, sit here, while we rest a bit."

3. *M. Le Poyntes:* "Sacré! Ze maid vill take ze child avay. Ze balloon annoy my chapeau."

4. *The Maid:* "Thot Oi will not! Take away yersilf, av ye don't be afther loikin' it. Shure it's not fer the loikes uv an ould Frinchy thot Oi'll be movin' on."

5. *(Aside.)* "Thot strong wind is goin' to blow th' balloon t' give him a good wan in th' oye!"

6. *But just then the balloon was blown hard against that pointedly-waxed moustache.*

7. *M. Le Poyntes:* "Ze barbair zat vaxed zat moustache know his business."

The British were usually portrayed as brave and noble:

'Boys!' he cried, 'we want more cartridges. There is an ammunition wagon in a donga just behind us across the valley. I want volunteers.'

Instantly the whole line sprang to its feet. Another British characteristic. The call for volunteers is never made in vain.

'One gains a wider conception of the Brotherhood of Man,' remarked Baden-Powell, 'where the hardship and dangers are shared by faithful, if less civilized, natives.' Foreigners, if not faithful natives, usually provided light relief. Comic French masters and 'Mamzelles' were a familiar ingredient of school stories; tales of adventure were embellished by such characters as 'Ching Lung: A Chinese Prince. He is an expert conjuror and always up to some fun', and 'Pierre Bovrille: A funny Frenchman'. If neither funny nor faithful, foreigners were often sinister:

No other nation, in my opinion, exists that can lie in the masterly fashion of the Chinese: and though the expression of his face did not change, nor yet bore too great an absence of expression, I knew like a shot, that Quon Main was lying.

There were collections of poems for children to recite, with more than their share of patriotism:

> Come, comrades, just one struggle
> And mastered is the shore,
> And these black fiends shall juggle
> With England's might no more...

and another:

> Boys, beneath your breath, speak softly honoured hero names, and
>   then
> Thank the God of every nation he hath made you Englishmen.

Stirring stuff, which made the 'hints to reciters' almost unnecessary:

Stamping should be be used very sparingly, and only in an angry passage; kneeling is useful in token of submission or prayer. Only kneel on one knee, however, and always keep half turned to the people, so that they may have the benefit of your face.... A quarter of an hour is quite long enough for a recitation.

Chapter Five
FAMILY AND FRIENDS

WITH GRANDMOTHER

A CHILD OLD ENOUGH TO COME
DOWNSTAIRS WAS EXPECTED
TO PLAY ITS PART

Mother: "Now, dear, why don't you run away and give Grandpa a kiss!"
Child (who can see nothing but Grandpapa's moustache and beard): "I don't see any place for it, Mamma!"

IT WAS TERRIFYING, BUT GOOD TRAINING

Thinking of myself, where I think our education was perhaps better than now was that we were expected to be at luncheon, and in a way we took part, and therefore we did hear quite a lot of good conversation. I think in that way we were less cut off from what was going on than one would be now. People today might be inclined to put the schoolroom children into the school-room for luncheon if the Prime Minister was lunching; in those days I think grown-ups and children mixed more together.

From the time a child was old enough to come downstairs he was expected to play his part. 'You wouldn't lunch downstairs until you were quite twelve or perhaps fourteen, because you had to be able to talk. If you didn't talk you got a raspberry from your mother afterwards, because there was silence where you were sitting. I'm talking about when there were guests. It was terrifying, but good training. To this day I can say this with truth, I've never had sticky silences at my table.'

In some houses the younger children, when they first came down to lunch, were put at a separate table:

There was me and my sister and two cousins and perhaps two others, at the end of the room, and we jawed away about food and anything else. The high-class conversation, such as it was, went on at the other table. Then, later you were put next to a kindly guest, in a party of about eight, probably. The thing you did learn was never, never to interrupt. That got you into real trouble. But you were quite smiled upon if the conversation dropped and you said, 'Mama!' in a high voice, 'I saw a horse run away this morning,' and everyone would say 'Did you really? What happened?' That was a good mark; it started things up again. My mother used to say, 'If you have a hole at a luncheon party, it can spoil it all.' By 'a hole' she meant a silent person. But I think you got into trouble if you talked without thinking. You had to have something to say.

Manners were the great thing [said Lady Remnant]. My sister and I always had tea in a small sitting room which was handed over to us, but then after tea we went into the drawing room, to Grandmother, and everyone was there. And my goodness, you were always being told about your manners. I remember my grandmother saying to me, 'When you come into the room, it doesn't matter if you've never seen the people before, go straight up, hold out your hand and say "how do you do?" – and *look* them in the face.' My grandmother knew everyone and she would go out calling. She drove in her high dogcart and generally my aunt went too and sat beside her. I sat on a little narrow seat at the back, with my back to them. Frightfully uncomfortable; I did not enjoy it at all. She used to leave cards and sometimes went in. It was more or less every day she went calling, because you *had* to return cards and you *had* to call on anyone new that arrived.

I think children were taught good manners then, more than now [said Grizel Hartley]. I was always told that you were put into this world to see

that other people were comfortable and happy and had all they wanted, and only after all that could you start thinking about yourself.

The message was driven home by the reading matter considered suitable for children. *Sunday Reading for the Young*, for example, in 1904 featured an article on good manners:

Chats with Children
Good Manners

'The well-mannered child no longer exists – it is as extinct as the Dodo,' was the remark I one day heard from the lips of a great lady.

It was a sweeping remark – not altogether true, but there is *some* truth in it, alas!

The children of today are not monsters. They are more helpful, intelligent and thoughtful, especially towards the poor, than were the children of half a century ago, but their manners are certainly not so good. The gentle speech and pretty ways which used to be the characteristic of a well-born child are fast disappearing from among us.

'Politeness,' says an old writer, 'may be compared to an air cushion. There is nothing much in it, but it is very useful in guarding us from the rough corners of life.'

A FAMILY OUTING

Try then, children of this twentieth century, to see if you cannot acquire the good manners which are so fascinating both in young and old.

For instance, when strangers leave your mother's drawing room, do not wait to be told to open the door for them, but jump up of your own accord, and hold open the door with a pleasant smile. The action which costs you so little will be remembered by them when you have long forgotten it.

Another lapse in manners is often made which perhaps a hint may prevent. If you write to anyone who is staying away from their own home, do not direct to your friend as if the house he or she happens to be staying at belonged to them. If your sister is staying with her aunt at Oakleigh Hall, do not direct, 'Miss Laura Norman, Oakleigh Hall, Exeter,' but put 'Miss Laura Norman, Care of Mrs Rolleston, etc., etc.'

This is a proper compliment to the owner of the house, and should never be omitted.

Whilst on the subject of letters let me warn you not to make remarks on even the outsides of any letters that others may receive. Do not say, 'Look at that seal on Uncle's letter,' or, 'What a long letter Miss Smith has got.' Take no notice of anyone's letter but your own, and if you are asked to fetch the letters from the post box do not deal them round to their owners, but carry them all to the mistress of the house, and wait for her to give them to you to take to their owners.

Never forget to shut the door when you leave the room, and shut it quietly. See if Grannie has a foot-stool, or if anyone wants a message delivered, and try to be kind and helpful, and then we shall no longer hear that the race of well-mannered children is extinct.

Another aspect of manners was 'the things one simply didn't talk about'. One of these was age:

Age was absolute taboo; it was never mentioned. Nobody knew how old my grandmother was, my aunts were, my mother was. Age was never referred to, and as for celebrating your fortieth birthday as everyone does now, it never ever happened.

'NOBODY KNEW HOW OLD MY MOTHER WAS'

Children learned to avoid other subjects which shocked grown-ups:

I was very jealous of my brother, who was eighteen months younger than I was. We were in our pram, and somebody or other said, 'Oh, what a dear little boy, what a lovely baby!' So I said, darkly, 'You should see the other end!' It stopped the conversation at once.

Any child who dropped a brick would not forget it in a hurry:

I remember when I was about ten I went to a rather grand garden party in Chelsea. My father's cousin had been in India, where he had recently married and he'd just come back with his bride. I was in a group of Edwardian ladies and gentlemen who were talking about this and saying, in that way they did, 'Who *was* she?' And I said, in ringing tones that could have been heard in Westminster, 'I believe she was a garrison hack.' I always remember the stunned silence, and then peals and peals of laughter. The silence seemed to last and last like a wave that's going to break. And the terrible trouble I got into – where had I heard this, and so on.

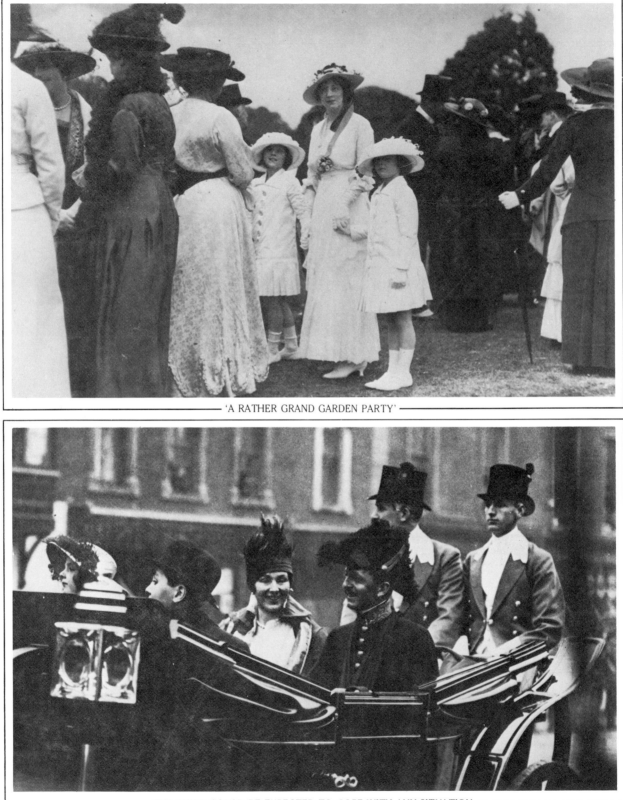

'A RATHER GRAND GARDEN PARTY'

THE CHILD COULD BE EXPECTED TO COPE WITH ANY SITUATION:
RIDING THROUGH DUBLIN IN A STATE COACH

Having learned how to behave, the child could be expected to cope with any situation. Victoria Dane used to go with her parents to stay with the Duchess of Fife:

She insisted. She said, 'Victoria must come too.' I was a little girl, about eleven or twelve, and I shall never forget the Princess Royal saying, 'Victoria must come down to dinner because she will like to hear the piper playing,' and Mother saying, 'Now, you know, you'll have to eat off silver plates, and you *must* be careful not to make them squeak.' So down I came to dinner, terrified, in a little dress with a sash. I sat on a cushion because I was too small to reach the table, terrified that I was going to make my knife squeak on the silver plates; it's terrible, eating off silver plates. At last there was the piper, piping round, at the end, and I was allowed to go to bed.

Even more alarming were the visits of Lord Kitchener to Victoria's Scottish home:

My dear, I was terrified of him. I'll never forget the last time he came to stay. I suppose I was about twelve, and my friend Kathleen was staying at the time. Kathleen danced most beautifully, so Mother said, 'Now, you've got to do something to amuse Lord Kitchener.' So Kathleen dressed up as a kind of Spaniard with curtain rings in her ears and she did a most wonderful dance, and I had to recite 'The Revenge'. In those days you did things like that, played the piano and recited; everything was much more simple, then. We did a little play that we had invented in the afternoon, Kathleen danced Spanish dances and I just shouted 'The Revenge', and that was our entertainment. And, do you know, he was thrilled! He really was. He told my mother afterwards, 'Nothing like this has ever happened to me before and I have so enjoyed it.' What was terrifying about him was the eye that didn't look at you. You see, in his youth his brother had shot an arrow into his eye by mistake, and so his eye wandered and didn't really look at you, which was rather intimidating. He was a very tall man, of course, very big; a handsome man in a way. Great moustache. But you never knew when he was looking at you and when he wasn't.

'YOU'VE GOT TO DO SOMETHING TO AMUSE LORD KITCHENER'

Grown-ups were very good in those days; they never spoke to a child in an inferior way [said the Dowager Duchess of Devonshire]. If a child was at lunch, he was treated the same way as everyone else and his opinion was taken the same as anyone else's. People like Arthur Balfour were wonderful, because they always brought you in. He had very good manners, and he'd say, 'Now, what do you think, my dear?' and you were absolutely paralysed, probably hadn't been thinking about anything except your horse, but that was what he always did. It had this advantage, that if you knew that at some agonizing moment someone was going to ask you what you thought you really did listen to what was going on, and therefore you did learn. We learned from conversation some general knowledge; we heard on Tuesday, at luncheon, about what was happening in, say, Iceland and that left a sediment of information about Iceland. I think the very good-mannered people in my time, if the child was twelve or fourteen, would turn and say, 'What do you think about it, my dear?' about tariff reform, or whatever was being talked about. They'd bring you in.

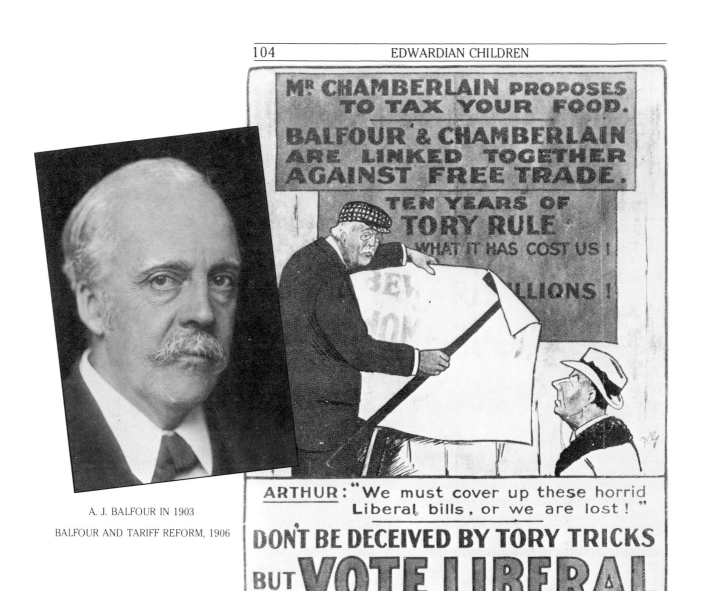

A. J. BALFOUR IN 1903

BALFOUR AND TARIFF REFORM, 1906

I never read a book [said the son of a Norfolk squire]. None of my family ever read a book. No book had been added to the library since 1820. But I used to listen to the conversation. Of course, we weren't allowed to speak, but I used to listen to all the interesting people who came to the house, like Grey and Kitchener, at shooting lunches.

There was a great deal of hospitality, and not only in the grand houses:

My father was a champion draughts player and we used to have draughts parties, all those little baize tables all laid out. I can play draughts now, and I don't think you can beat me yet! We used to have a singsong – my piano teacher used to come and play the piano. The cousins were always welcome when they came to the house. There was always a good tea, tons of food all laid out, scones and cakes and this, that and the other. Everybody was welcome. The minister used to come about twice a week

and sit and have a glass of sherry and a homemade cake, at eleven o'clock in the morning. Later, when we lived in Aberdeen, my stepmother's nephew, who had a large farm, used to come in every Friday, with his wife; they brought chickens, and flowers, and eggs and cream. Then he went to the market and she went shopping and we took in all their messages and parcels all day long. The bell would ring all day, on Fridays, with those messenger boys coming. I used to love opening the door to all those lads and taking the parcels in. They'd come back about four o'clock and have a good tea and be off.

Family ties were very strong. In a small community the aunts, uncles and cousins were a very important part of a child's life:

My father came from a farming family. The eldest brother had the farm, so my father became a brewer. But he was a champion ploughman, he used to win all the cups. I can remember walking out with his dinner, when he was

'WE USED TO HAVE A SINGSONG'

ploughing. His sisters I do remember, they were my aunts and they all lived in Fraserburgh. There were so many of them and lots of cousins. The only one I remember was the disgraceful one, Maggie. When she was about sixteen she became pregnant, and that was a disgrace for a family in those days, you know. She had to leave, of course. Her mother was in a terrible state about it. But she married later on and she was very, very happy. My mother's family were all trawlermen, a different community altogether. They stayed in a different part of Fraserburgh, and to go in was like going into a little village; they were all fisher people, very simple people, but very good. They all went trawling; I used to go out with my cousins. There were so many herring that the fishermen used to throw them out on the beach, and the poor people used to go with a pail and pick them up; they lived on the herring.

I was in and out of my aunts' houses, all the time. It was nice, being with my mother's brothers and sisters – and with my father's. But they didn't mix, the fisher people and the country people. The fisher people were very narrow-minded, very religious – perhaps because of the sea. But all the clever children went to high school; they didn't want that life at all. None of my father's family managed that farm. Nobody managed the farm at all. They all went to universities and trained as teachers, that sort of thing, and they all scattered. The fisherfolk all went to Canada; they all went away. When the herring industry was failing there was nothing for them to do.

'NATURALLY, YOU WERE AWARE OF EMPIRE.' MAXIM GUN DETACHMENT, 1ST BN KINGS ROYAL RIFLES, CHITRAL CAMPAIGN, 1895

Other families scattered as a matter of course; they went out to run the Empire:

All those boys. I can't tell you how many relations I had, in things called Gardiner's Horse, or Skinner's Horse. It was absolutely taken for granted that one of the sons would go into the Indian Army or whatever it was.

Naturally you were aware of empire [said Judith Lyttelton]. Three-quarters of the world was coloured pink and in every port the majority of ships were flying the British flag. I think there are more English working in

India now than there were in our day, but it's not the same feeling. Then India was ours, and our relations went out there as a matter of duty. The white man's burden loomed very large. And it was very glorious. One didn't boast about it but one knew that it was there. I think perhaps we were more aware because of being Clives, and Clive's portrait was in the dining room.

Leila Hampden's Uncle Jim was a cavalry man in the Indian Army; and there was also Uncle Tom of the Egyptian police. He

waged war constantly and daringly against that most evil, yet profitable enterprise, the secret trafficking in drugs, especially hashish. It thrilled us to hear how often this was found in the padding of camel bags.

'Edwardians all wrote letters; everyone spent all the morning writing letters. They were writing to all their relations.' In big houses every bedroom had a writing table and many a child

'EDWARDIANS ALL WROTE LETTERS'

remembers going round with a basket, replenishing supplies of writing paper and envelopes and refilling ink wells and blotters. Often the unmarried aunts were the best correspondents, because they were expected to live at home until they married:

My aunt always had lived at home, looking after my grandmother. When I left school she thought it would be a very good idea if I went on the stage. It was the time of musical comedy and she thought that would be nice, and she thought that a job would be a good idea. That was remarkable, because women just didn't have jobs.

'WOMEN JUST DIDN'T HAVE JOBS'

AN EDWARDIAN MOTHER

Unmarried aunts were therefore available to bring up nieces and nephews whose parents were overseas and to look after their ageing mothers, 'wrapped up like Queen Victoria in a scarf and widow's weeds'. Old ladies

always wore a long black dress to the ground, with a very tight bodice, high to the neck. My grandmother always wore a lace cap. Even towards the end of her life, when she was unwell and in bed, she wore a cap. My aunt used to do her hair for her; it was thin and very little of it. My aunt would scrape it into a bun, and on top was this lovely lace cap. That was what everybody of her age would wear. I don't know what my grandmother would have done without my aunt, and she was marvellous to us, although it must have been a frightful bore to her to have us children always.

Isolation and leisure put nothing into people. But they give what is there full play. They allow it to grow according to itself and that may be strongly in certain directions. I am sure that the people who were middle-aged and elderly when I was young were more individualized than my own contemporaries are now . The effect of wider intercourse and self-adaptation seems to go below the surface and the result is that the essence of people is controlled and modified.

That was the opinion of Ivy Compton-Burnett. Certainly there was a good deal of eccentricity around. My great aunt remembered her Uncle Albert as

immensely tall, immensely thin, dressed in threadbare clerical clothes, bearded and unkempt, unlike anyone else in appearance or conversation. . . . When Guy and I were engaged [they married in 1905] he came to dinner and suddenly reared his gaunt form and addressed Guy: 'Which *cocoa* do you prefer; Fry's, Van Houten's, Cadbury's?' 'Does he think I travel in cocoa?' Guy asked, amazed. His wedding present to me was a nib – gold, it is true – in a matchbox; but this was better than his present to another of the family; one of his strange oil paintings rolled round so that it stuck together.

AN EDWARDIAN FATHER

Another eccentric parson was Leila Hampden's grandfather;

the last of the great sporting parsons. At the village fête he put on his boxing gloves and for sixpence anyone could have a go at pushing the rector into the ha-ha.

The Dowager Duchess of Devonshire described her aunt 'TT':

She was very clever, extremely eccentric. Time meant absolutely nothing to her. There came an awful day when she got very ill and she was almost dying. The family was in a terrible state about it, and a doctor was sent for. He turned to the maid who looked after her and he said, 'What has she been eating in the last day or two? It might be she has got some poison.' 'Oh, she hasn't.' 'How are you so sure?' 'Well her ladyship hasn't eaten *anything* for the last two or three days.' She recovered; they filled her up with food. She had simply forgotten to eat.

Richard Lyttelton's aunts

were only just stopped from sawing off the edges of all the Chippendale tables, those raised edges. They thought they were hideously in the way, which they are, of course, when you come to think of it.

In the closer family circle, fathers were often more companionable than mothers. Mothers were apt to spend a great deal of time doing 'The Books':

THE AUTHOR'S MOTHER (*RIGHT*), WITH HER SISTER AND PARENTS

There was a little book for each shop that you dealt with, and the cook used to trot up with The Books so that you could see what you had spent and sign the cheques. Doing The Books was one of the chatelaine's jobs, certainly once a week. And every day you ordered the meals. In London we would go to see my mother and she would say, 'Will you call Mrs Dobson?' and we would go to the top of the stairs and call out, 'Mrs Dobson! Mother wants you,' and up Mrs Dobson would come with a slate, with the meals of the day.

Fathers tended to lead a more active outdoor life:

My father was quite anxious about his estate, and we used to ride out every day. I think this was probably true of many, many families. My father saw the agent every week. He would say, 'So-and-so's chimney is smoking; they're having trouble with it – they probably need a new one.' So as I got on my pony at eleven o'clock, missing the German lesson which was supposed to be on, my father would decide to go to the cottage to see for himself. We always went to one cottage or another. When we came home my father would tell the agent what needed to be done. Probably this was the regular custom of a landlord in those days. If someone was ill, my father would be told, perhaps by the clergyman or the land agent or the district nurse, and the next morning my father would say, 'I must go to such-and-such a cottage; the man's been taken ill.' There was more actual, personal knowledge on a well-run estate – the landlord saw

A POOR FAMILY, 1910

everything for himself. That's how it was done, and on the whole it worked very well. Of course, let's be fair; if it was a very big estate, then it did depend tremendously on the land agent. It wouldn't be possible for the landlord to go personally to everybody – he'd go occasionally but not always. But my father used to go and visit all the farms, always. All the good landlords were in touch, unless the estate was very big. I know my father went out every day and nearly every day he would visit somebody. And I have no doubt he was the ordinary, average, conscientious landlord.

Separated from their children by nannies and boarding schools, some parents became very formidable. As the sister of one beloved but intimidating Edwardian father said regretfully:

I wish we could have been less afraid of him. I think he never realized how portentous was the effect of his disapproval. . . . He held that one must be inexorably truthful, however difficult truth made it for others. It was wrong to smile sympathetically at a joke that did not amuse you; wrong to help in the conversation by assuming a little knowledge, or at least interest. Nothing brought conversation to a fuller stop than his 'I know nothing whatever about it', when someone had ventured a remark on, say, India.

The little frictions and necessary adjustments of family life barely existed:

It was made quite clear to English children that from the time they were born they lived behind the baize door – we always had baize doors to muffle the nursery noises – and at the top of the house preferably. At eight you went to school and if you lived in the north of England they nearly always found a school in the south, and vice versa.

The system did not, of course, drive a wedge between children and parents who found it easy to enjoy their company. Catherine Staples, for example,

lived a very Edwardian life with a very efficient nanny and a nurserymaid. We lived in the nursery and we saw our parents twice a day, in the morning and in the evening. We used to go down to the schoolroom and then back to the nursery when our lessons were finished. We were kept in the nursery incredibly late, until we were about thirteen, and we didn't come down to dinner until we were grown-up. But we were very devoted to our parents. My father was a darling; every evening in the winter we took it in turns to go down to his study and we played games with him, cribbage or backgammon, the games he had taught us.

My father was a quite well-known architect; Frederick Hyde Pownall, his name was. Corpus Christi, Maiden Lane, was one of his churches. It kept its centenary two years ago and my sister and I went up to London. That was the church where I was married. We were devoted to our mother too. She was very pretty, lively, fond of society. The nanny didn't at all take the place of my mother – I wasn't very fond of her, actually. My father was

THE AUTHOR'S MOTHER IN HER CAR

much older than my mother and he died in 1907. I remember his funeral. We were quite ordinary people, not terribly important – my father was a very charming old man, that was all – but his funeral was something unbelievable, one of the last of those Edwardian funerals. I remember it so well; the whole of the station yard was full of those awful carriages with black horses, and all the traffic was stopped between Richmond and Mortlake because of the funeral going through.

WASHING DOLLS' CLOTHES

When my mother died [said Mabel Walker], everybody, all the women with their shawls, they were standing down the road for miles, crying and carrying on. She was always doing things to help the poor; she gave them clothes, and food. There were such poor people then, in the days of tinkers and gypsies and barrel organ men. The day she died, I was in the garden bleaching my little dollies' clothes, putting them in the sun to make them white, as the grown-ups used to do in those days, and I remember Chrissie, the nurserymaid, coming out into the garden and lifting me up, and saying, 'Mummy's died. You have to come in.' I was about six, and I remember my sister, Jessie, standing sobbing and my brother was saying, 'Dinna greet, Jessie, dinna greet.' My life changed altogether, when my mother died.

Chapter Six
TIME OFF

PLAYING 'DIABOLO'

'THERE WAS A LOT OF PULLING UP THE WINDOW ... WHENEVER WE WENT THROUGH A TUNNEL'

Cool nights, space, freedom, familiar welcoming faces, the beech tree to climb, the hammock under the limes to swing in, fruit to eat, the brothers' homecoming from school . . . I wish I could recapture for you a smallest part of the rapture of the summer exodus from London.

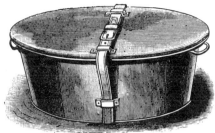

TRAVELLING BATH

We took a tremendous lot of luggage [said my father]. There was a tin bath, brown with a lid and a strap round it, which made an extra trunk. I think you did have to take your bath with you. We took a lot of clothes because nothing was drip-dry and when things were washed they had to be washed properly; although it was a seaside holiday we would certainly be expected to be properly dressed.

If you were going to move your whole family – that would be three children in our case, a nurse and a nurserymaid and possibly somebody else, with all their luggage, it paid you, instead of having a cab, or a fly, or a four-wheeler to hire a horse-drawn bus provided by the railway company. You hired it from the station, it was part of the service. We would set out with all our luggage on the roof of this bus. Coming home, my recollection is that one or two men would run alongside our bus, so as to get a tip for unloading – they lay in wait at Victoria Station. Of course, they wouldn't have known where we were going. It wasn't far from Victoria to our house, but I suppose if we'd been going to Hampstead or somewhere they might possibly have given up hope when we got into Roseberry Avenue.

All the trains were steam, of course, and there was a lot of pulling up the window, with its big leather strap, whenever we went through a tunnel. We very often travelled with the cousins and then there would be seven children, two nannies and two nurserymaids – and a good deal of jollity.

PADDINGTON STATION

It was a very long journey to Happisburgh. I don't know how we were kept amused. When we got to North Walsham, which was the station, we were met by Mr Clements in what we called 'the pillbox', a sort of brougham. The drive seemed absolutely interminable; it was seven miles and it took an hour, perhaps. Norfolk was so remote in those days. I'll tell you the kind of thing – a man used to come round with a dancing bear, I remember that quite well.

SEASIDE HUMOUR, 1913

TOWN FULL BUT HAVE GOT SOME WELL AIRED BEDS.

THE COWES FERRY, ISLE OF WIGHT

BURNHAM SANDS

Every year we went on our summer holidays, [said Catherine Staples]. At first it was always Littlehampton, for years, and later the Isle of Wight. My parents came too. We generally took rooms; we went back to the same house year after year. We didn't take a cook with us. The people of the house cooked for us, I think, but in those days the children of the house didn't have anything to do with the domestic arrangements. We were only allowed into the kitchen once a year, and that was to stir the Christmas pudding.

We wore incredible bathing dresses which were made by our nurse. I remember mine so well: blue serge, and it came down to the knees, with a coat which buttoned up to the neck, with an anchor on it, which we thought very *sportif*. We had a coastguard who used to try to teach us to swim. He, poor man, walked up and down in the water with anyone who wanted to have swimming lessons. Anyhow, he never succeeded in teaching me to swim, but I loved the water.

There were bathing machines, drawn down into the water by a horse. I remember the thrill of the smell of those bathing machines. They were perfectly clean but they smelt fusty and seasidey and there was straw or sawdust on the floor. You dressed and undressed in the bathing machine and came down some little steps into the water. The horse was brought in as the sea receded, when the tide was going out, to tow your bathing machine back into the sea. It was a wonderful idea.

'MAGICAL MARGATE' (POSTER, 1907)

HATS ON THE BEACH

'THE YORKSHIRE PIERROTS AND FRED PULLIN', CLACTON-ON-SEA

'THERE WERE BATHING MACHINES'

Other children went further afield. Grizel Hartley went to Scotland, where

we had a house on Loch Fyne, which was an absolutely wonderful place to go. It wasn't at all a grand house; it was rather shabby and comfortable. We went on a lovely train, and then on a sort of horse-drawn charabanc for the last eighteen miles. There wasn't a station any nearer. The children were always made to get out and walk up the hills, to spare the horses. When we were there, we used to get about by foot, or by pony, or bicycle, but we had to do the shopping by sailing dinghy, which was rather nice, because the nearest shop was two miles away across the water. It was paradise.

Lady Remnant used to go to her uncle's house in Ireland:

It was in County Mayo, away in the west of Ireland, a quite small, old house with the most beautiful ceilings – but no water. Everything was fetched in a bucket. You had a tin bath in your bedroom and you were brought water to bath in, and to wash.

'YOU TOOK A CAB FROM THE STATION'

SAILING IN SCOTLAND, AUGUST 1909

Twickenham, where Catherine Staples lived, was then a village by the river:

Between Twickenham and Richmond, which was the nearest big place, the only transport was a horse bus with straw spread on the floor, and that went twice a day. York Street, which is now the big main road between Twickenham and Richmond, didn't exist. Where York Street now starts, there was a big chestnut tree with a seat all round it, where all the old men sat and smoked their pipes in the evening. The whole way between Twickenham and Isleworth, all the way along, was nothing but orchards.

So, as a change from the rural life of Twickenham, her yearly treat was to go to London, to stay with a friend whose father was a doctor in Wimpole Street:

We used to set out with our nurse, and our luggage was what was called a 'pilgrim basket'. It was two baskets that fitted into each other; everything was put in, and as it went in the basket grew higher and higher. It was done up with straps. You just relied on porters, and you took a cab from the station. I remember my first ride in a taxi, about this period. That was a tremendous excitement.

TELEPHONES WERE JUST COMING IN; A TELEPHONE EXCHANGE IN ABOUT 1900

It was in this house in Wimpole Street that Catherine Staples first saw a telephone.

There was a telephone in the surgery, the first I had ever seen. This was about 1903. My sister and I and our friend all got into the surgery when the doctor was out one day, and we thought we would have a little fun with the telephone. I looked up the number in the directory and I rang up a livery stable man whose name was Wheel. When he answered I said, 'Is your name Wheel? Because mine is Catherine and I think it would be so lovely to be Mrs Catherine Wheel!' I remember that very well. At that moment the doctor came back and was furious with us, of course.

In our family we were too poor, I think, to travel out together [said Mrs Huxley]. My father was the manager of a gents' outfitting shop in Ashford and we were ten children. It was a very happy childhood; there was never very much money but we were all very happy and we remained a very united family. My parents were very fair; if they couldn't afford to pay for all of us to go, then none of us could go. No one in the family was treated any different from another. But the Sunday school treats, they were marvellous. We used to go out into the country sometimes, into the fields, and we had sports and games and all sorts of things – quite a highday.

SCHOOL TREATS OFTEN INCLUDED SPORTS AND DANCES

Sometimes we went to the sea; I remember going to Hythe and Sandgate and having a day by the seaside, and of course that was great. We used to go on the railway and the first time I think we went to Whitstable, and I was sick because of the smell of the sea; that was one thing I couldn't stand. Probably the train had something to do with it, because I was always a dreadful traveller.

There were the carriers' vans but the trains were the greatest means of travel in those days. The country roads were dreadful for dust. Oh, it was terrible; the hedges were white, if you had a dry spell, and dust was everywhere. We did a lot of walking; the only way of getting to places was to walk. It was about 1900, when I was about fourteen, that I had my first bicycle; I learned to ride on a bone-shaker, with thin, hard, rubber tyres. They really were bone-shakers, but we used to have great fun. You still used to see the pennyfarthing bicycles on the road.

When it was fair time in Ashford, there would be a big procession through the town with elephants and all the other animals. And there were men on great big stilts; if you were at a bedroom window looking out,

A BICYCLING CATALOGUE

'THE CYCLISTS' REST' AT COBHAM, SURREY

GET A CAESAR CYCLE
Will take you there & bring you back everytime safely
—FIVE YEARS' GUARANTEE—

GENT'S £6·12·6

Dunlop, Palmer, or Clincher A1 Tyres, two Crabbe Inverted Lever Rim Brakes, Hyde Free Wheel, Brooks' Saddle, finished black, and lined in two colours.

WRITE FOR LIST AND EASY PAYMENT TERMS.

CAESAR CYCLE CO., LTD., COVENTRY.

PUNCH AND JUDY

DANCING TO THE MUSIC OF A STREET ORGAN

you could put your money in the boxes they carried – they were collecting money as they went along. It was great fun when the fairs came to the town, and the circuses. Steam organs, they were lovely, and the round-abouts. But I don't think that we ever actually went to the fair, because if all ten of us couldn't go, none could go.

I used to trundle my hoop all the way to school, because there wasn't very much traffic. There were seasons when we had tops, and then I would whip a top from home to school – I suppose it was about twenty minutes' walk. The boys used to trundle their iron hoops, and they had what they called a 'skid', which was a wooden handle with a piece of metal which went round with a hook on the end. The girls had wooden hoops with a wooden stick. I used to love to get my brother's iron hoop; it made such a lovely noise.

We played in the road, and just pulled up if a horse came by. We used to walk on stilts, and play tipcat, and fivestones – we used to play that with bones from a leg of lamb, I think it was. We used to clean the bones and play with them: they were smoother than stones. We played 'The Happy Miller'; that was a singing game, played standing in a ring. We played a lot of those kind of games, singing games, like 'Poor Jenny Sits A-Weeping' and 'Ring of Roses'.

TRUNDLING A HOOP. RAVEN HILL, 1900

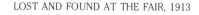

LOST AND FOUND AT THE FAIR, 1913

Families were much bigger then, and when there was a wedding or a christening, they were great highlights. Christmas was a family party, great fun, with games. We didn't have much in the way of presents – there wasn't the money for that – but I think we appreciated far more what we had than children do today. I remember one Easter, one of my sister's young men came and he brought me a little bottle of scent inside an Easter egg; I was about fourteen then, and I thought it was wonderful.

Now, by the time children are thirteen or fourteen they've had the lot, and nothing short of a motorbike, or their own television, will do for a present for them. But we used to make our own fun.

Later, when the children were earning, there was a little more money for treats:

Two or three of us girls would go to London and have a chicken supper at Fleming's; that was a rather nice restaurant. It was a great evening out. We

DERBY DAY, IN STYLE

A FAMILY AT THE RACES

DERBY DAY; THE FRUITERER'S CART

GEORGE ROBEY

GOING TO THE THEATRE

DOUBLE BILL AT THE NEW THEATRE,
1908

went to the theatre afterwards, not the music halls – they weren't good places for girls to go. There was music at Selfridges. I remember that there was a very nice tenor that we used to like to hear at Selfridges, and I think we could have supper there, too.

Grizel Hartley, on the other hand, loved the music hall:

A great treat was to go to the London Coliseum. It was the old-fashioned music hall, with the turns and the numbers put up in red or green lights at the side – Chinese jugglers, or trick cyclists, or a short play. It was absolute heaven.

It was there that she saw Vesta Tilley, in her top-hat and tails. 'Today people would think there was something awfully sinister about her, wouldn't they?' Vesta Tilley sang:

VESTA TILLEY

> 'He's very well-known is Algy, to the ladies on the stage;
> Such a jolly good chap is Algy, just now he's all the rage;
> Such a jolly big favourite, Algy, with the barmaids at the 'Cri'
> He's very well-known is Algy
> As the Piccadilly Johnny with the little glass eye.'

By 1904 there were no fewer than sixteen main music halls in operation in London alone. As Neville Cardus wrote in *Full Score*:

In my youth, around 1905, the music hall was abundant, a mirror held up to the life and habits of the nation, notably reflecting the joys, trials and domestic frustrations of the 'lower classes'. In every large city a Moss or Stolls Empire or Hippodrome was erected . . . into these new Empires and Hippodromes of plush and gilt, the family could respectably venture

There they might see Marie Lloyd as though leaning over the gold bar of heaven, beer-pumps of paradise beside her. She would sing and tell us that 'our lodger's such a nice young man. . . . He's so sweet, so very, very sweet – mother tells me so.' All sung and acted with glances and gestures of unprintable imputations.

Every week Cardus and his friends would eagerly scan the hoardings in Manchester to see what entertainments were in store for them:

LITTLE TICH

A small company of us boys, housed in bathless, unlavatoried houses in Rusholme and Moss Side, would go to the Tivoli gallery. We saved weekly from our earnings as carriers and fetchers, handcart pullers, sub-clerks, newspaper sellers in the streets, and before invading the Tivoli we 'clubbed' our financial assets and bought a supply of eggs, sharing them equitably.

The eggs were for throwing at unfunny comedians. Was this the reason why there were so many who were so funny? These were vintage years. There was the waif-like George Formby, George Robey with his eyebrows, his suggestive songs and his look of pained surprise when the audience grasped the double-entendre, and there was Little Tich, perhaps the funniest of them all, bowing so low that he knocked himself out, and making the ten-year-old Cardus laugh 'so convulsively that I fell off my seat at the Manchester Palace Theatre'.

Pantomime, then as now, was not always a pleasure:

My sister didn't like the pantomimes; she wanted them to get on with the story. So did I, really, but as everybody laughed at the comedians I thought I had better laugh too. I do remember one joke, not really aimed at children: 'Let's take a taxi.' 'There are no taxis – only Lloyd George's Taxes!' I laughed my head off; I didn't think it funny, but I wasn't going to be left out.

PRINCIPAL GIRL, JACK,
DRESSED IN SCOUT'S UNIFORM

JACK AND THE BEANSTALK

Musical comedy was better. Victoria Dane remembers the first time she went to a musical: it was *The Arcadians* in 1910. This was an immensely successful show which opened in 1909 with Phyllis Dare as the leading lady; it ran in London for two and a half years and then toured the provinces with its catchy overture, 'I've Gotter Motter – always Merry and Bright', and the 'Shower Chorus' with its neat rhymes:

> See our dresses – every one done
> By the foremost firms in London,
> All their handiwork is undone, every shred.
> Swan from Edgar swims asunder,
> Stagg has got her mantle under,
> Pooles in puddles slip and blunder, hope is fled.

THE ARCADIANS

GERALD DU MAURIER

In a class of its own was *Peter Pan*. Rupert Brooke wrote in a letter:

It was perfect. It is merely and completely the incarnation of all one's childish dreams – and the best dreams, almost, that one has. Red Indians, a Pirate Captain, Faeries, and all mixed up with Home. . . . It is wonderfully refreshing, and never silly . . . Gerald du Maurier as the Pirate Captain was perfect.

PETER PAN 1907: HILDA TREVELYAN AS
WENDY

CECILIA LOFTUS AS PETER PAN

Grizel Hartley remembers Gerald du Maurier:

He had so much charm, it wasn't possible. And it wasn't the Noel Coward sort of charm; it was much more straightforward. In those days mothers were very anxious that their children should hear all the best music and see the best actors. I was taken to Melba and Tetrazzini, and I even saw Sarah Bernhardt. Although she was old – she was acting in *L'Aiglon* – and I believe she had a wooden leg by then, it was undoubtedly something to remember.

SARAH BERNHARDT (*right*) 'WAS UNDOUBTEDLY SOMETHING TO REMEMBER'

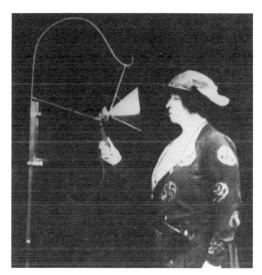

NELLIE MELBA IN HER LATER YEARS

Grizel Hartley was fortunate in having parents and neighbours who were interested in the arts. Their neighbours in Hammersmith were, on one side, F.G. Stephens,

the last of the pre-Raphaelites – the one that no one has ever heard of. I think he only ever painted about one picture, but he was one of the original Brotherhood. We were very interested in all that, because my mother was very beautiful and she was always being asked to sit for somebody or other. On our other side was May Morris, who was William Morris's daughter; she used to make us little spoons and forks out of real silver for our dolls.

'FLYING AT HENDON' (LONDON TRANSPORT POSTER)

More middlebrow parents, who were not regular concert-goers, might take their children to hear the famous Clara Butt, massive in size (she was six feet two inches) and in voice, singing 'Abide With Me' and 'Land of Hope and Glory'. Clara Butt was the original of George du Maurier's *Trilby*; he wrote of her:

No such magnificent or seductive apparition has ever been seen before or since on any stage or platform. Her voice was so immense in its softness, richness, freshness that it seemed to be pouring itself out from all round; one felt it to be not only faultless, but infallible.

However, the young Neville Cardus was less reverent; after 'resonant Gluck', Clara Butt 'in deep tones, and capacious as a battleship, informed the audience that she would, as an encore, sing "Dear Little Jammy-Face". It was an age
of gloriously bad taste.'

AERIAL GREETINGS CARD, 1910

Small boys, my father among them, were taken to see the magnificent men in their flying machines at an air display at Hendon, and, even better, to the exhibition at the White City where

there was the Mountain Railway and Scenic Railway, but what I remember best was that there was a man demonstrating X-rays. This must have been appallingly dangerous. He said to me, 'Come along, sonny,' and so I was pushed forward by Cossie, and others. I stood in front of an admiring audience with a thing rather like a slate in front of me, and something was switched on behind. There was a green glow, and there were my ribs, and my buttons. There was a good deal of ribaldry about my buttons. 'Your nanny wants to sew on that button,' and then, 'That's your heart. Didn't know you *had* a heart, did you, son?' That was really exciting.

There was a great deal of visiting and hospitality which, according to their temperament, children found entertaining or the reverse. Some little girls enjoyed being dressed up for their mothers' 'At Home' days.

DRESSED UP FOR 'AT HOME' DAYS

Everybody arrived in their carriage, if they had a carriage. I remember there was an old lady who used to come, with a lovely pair of horses. The nurserymaid would say, 'Mrs Mackintosh has come with the pair' – and for years I thought she meant 'a pear' and was so disappointed not to see one. On the 'At Home' days, the nurserymaid was stationed at the window upstairs to see who was arriving and she would come and tell our nurse, who then dressed us all up and sent us down to the drawing room, looking perfectly sweet. It was impressed on me that I must never say anything about my clothes. But once I said to a visitor, stretching out my feet, 'Look! Pink shoes!' I've always remembered that because I knew, you see, that I was being naughty.

On dinner-party nights, 'the great excitement was to hang over the banisters with the housemaids, to watch the people going into dinner – but you couldn't allow yourself to be seen.' Older children were sometimes allowed to listen to the music after dinner, a doubtful treat:

Of course people were much less critical then but most of it was fairly excruciating. On one occasion a young lady began to play the piano and her mother stopped her and said, 'Play it more slowly, my dear – remember it's Sunday!'

MUSIC AFTER DINNER COULD BE 'FAIRLY EXCRUCIATING'

Better were the pickings from the grown-ups' feast:

There was a bachelor called Freddy Wallop who used to come and stay and he was sweet to children – he used to collect the preserved fruits off the dining-room table; we would call on him in the morning while he was still in bed and he had his pockets full of fruit for us.

Great was Victoria Dane's rage when

some people had come to dinner and the cook had made meringues – and she wouldn't give me one. So the next day I locked the cook in her bedroom at the top of the house and took the key and threw it away. I was a terribly naughty child. I was shut up all the next day in my bedroom, with bread and water.

There were children's parties:

You had a card for your partners, each with a little pink pencil. There was a huge tea, and then a conjurer and dancing. Then you went down to supper with little boys in Eton collars who would fetch you ice-cream.

A CHILDREN'S PARTY

Lady Remnant still remembers, sadly, a party to which she was not allowed to go:

There were some very rich people living in an enormous house at Ascot and one summer they gave a haymaking party for their children and they asked me. I was about six or seven at the time. My grandmother said that I was not to go because she didn't want to know them. They were 'in trade' and if my grandmother had wanted to know them she would have called. How extraordinary it all was!

A WEDDING PARTY

Catherine Staples remembers one very special party:

Our parlourmaid got married. She had been with us for years and she had no family or relations near because she had come over from Ireland and she was marrying an Irishman. So my father said she could be married from our house and they could have the servants' hall for their wedding breakfast. My brother, who was then aged about seven, was their best man, and my sister and I were the bridesmaids. There was no proper road then; it was just a lane between our house and the little Catholic church where they were married. After the wedding we all walked back, the bride and the bridegroom, my brother – the best man – and my sister and I, who were just little tots. I remember the gardeners of the house next door throwing rice over the wall as we went by. Then we had the wedding breakfast in the servants' hall. The bride had invited her friends, the tradespeople in the village. We children were allowed to go down. There was a young man there called Page, who was the draper. I was terribly smitten with this young man and I sat on his lap and was in a seventh heaven. It was lovely. And then in came my father, to drink their health in a glass of port.

Christmas was of course the highlight of the children's year:

It was tremendous fun. I don't quite know why, because the presents were very feeble, but there was a great feeling of excitement. There was always a big houseparty. On Christmas morning we used to go round and sing 'Hark, the Herald Angels Sing' outside the bedroom doors. My uncle

WINTRY WINDS

CHRISTMAS HOLIDAYS

always played up: you'd hear him say, 'Angels, surely!' and then, 'Come in.' The girls were always commissioned to take round 'The Bundles' to all the cottages. The Bundles consisted of yards of cloth and also joints of beef; they were given up, later, because they were thought to be patronizing, or out of date, anyway.

THE FROZEN RIVER AT HENLEY

NEW YEAR MEAT DISPLAY

Before the war, however, there was no hesitation in giving out Christmas joints to the entire estate. As Judith Lyttelton remembers:

Everyone was given meat at Christmas; it was all worked out by the agent; he knew exactly which family had ten children and must have a big sirloin, and which had only two children. I can still see those huge hunks of meat dripping with blood which had to be given out. And everyone had a whale of a time at the Christmas dances.

The 1900 Christmas poem of the magazine *Sphere*, first published in that year, struck the right note of anticipation with the obligatory moral warnings:

Santa Claus

Whether it freezes, whether it thaws,
Over the roofs comes Santa Claus,
   Driving his team
   Swift as a dream,
Jingle of bells in a cloud of steam!
He has a sleigh that's like the wind
Spite of the parcels piled behind –
   Goodies and toys
   Meant for the joys
Only of good little girls and boys.

   So the Saint,
   Queer and quaint,
Comes without ringing or knocking
   And he strews
   Down the flues
Gifts that you find in your stocking.

Marbles and nuts, the old man knows,
Fill up the room of tiny toes;
   Oranges feel
   Round as your heel,
Only their skin is a golden peel;
Boxes of sweets are neatly put
Down where you used to keep your foot;
   Soldiers of tin
   March up the shin –
How did he manage to get them in?

   But if you,
   Children, do
Anything naughty and shocking.
   Not a sweet
   You will meet –
Only the holes in your stocking.

Chapter Seven
GROWING UP

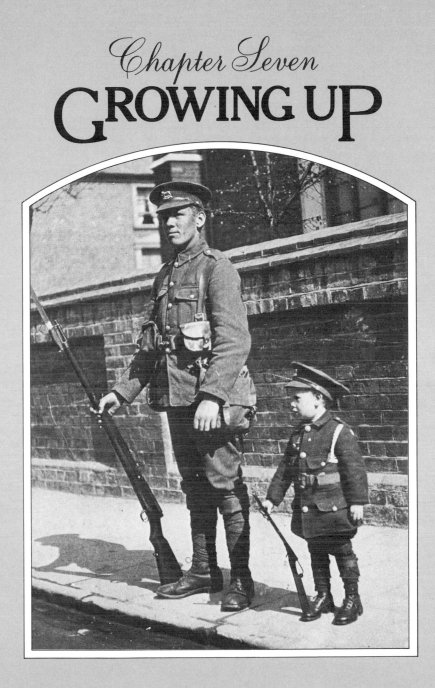

ENGINE DRIVER AND HIS MATE

'THERE THEY WERE, ALL THESE PARSONS'

People say, 'boys will be boys', but they are wrong   – boys will
be *men*. And to prepare for their manhood not a day is to be
lost. The weakling goes to the wall in the great battle of life.
('How to Succeed In Life: Some Finger-Posts for Boys', *Boy's
Own Paper*, 1910)

Although 99 per cent of boys wanted to become engine-
drivers, according to Baden-Powell, by the time the sons of
the gentry grew up their course was clear and set on
almost eighteenth-century lines:

I became a land agent because I already had a brother in the army and I
didn't want to be a parson, although it was a good thing to be a parson,
because there were so many livings. My father had several livings in his
gift, so of course if any niece married a parson there would always be a
living for her husband. So there they were, all these parsons, and they
could live very comfortably, in those days, on a few hundred a year.
However, I didn't want to go into the Church and I became a land agent. It
was a great help to me, the way I had been brought up, because I knew
how things were done and what went on. For example, I knew that at a
shoot the keeper has to be given not one but two bottles of whisky, that
kind of thing.

'THEY COULD LIVE VERY COMFORTABLY ... ON A FEW HUNDRED A YEAR'

THE NAVY: HMS *KING EDWARD VII*

The Army, the Navy, the Foreign Office, politics, the Bar; these were almost the only professions thought suitable for gentlemen. Solicitors, doctors and clergymen were on the borderline. 'The money instinct' struck Judith Lyttelton immediately when she stayed in America as a girl of seventeen:

All the young men you met there were going into the City. There was never any question of the Army or the Foreign Office or anything like that, in the days when, in England, it was quite rare to do anything else. We could have done with a mixture, couldn't we? It was too much the other way, here.

Lady Remnant remembers that when she married a stockbroker,

my grandmother, though she loved him, wasn't at all happy at his being a stockbroker. The City didn't come into life at all. My parents wouldn't have felt like that, but my grandmother did. Although he had been to Eton, and his father was an MP and a baronet, she wasn't at all happy about him being in the City.

The choice was even more simple for the daughters, for most of them were expected to do nothing at all until they married:

I never remember having any ambitions when I was a child. People just didn't have jobs. None of my friends, that is the girls, none of them had jobs. I always did the flowers, I loved doing that, but that was all. I wasn't bored; I had a lovely time with friends and so on, but it never occurred to me to have a job.

Catherine Staples was sent to a finishing school in Belgium for a
year, to learn French, and then to another in Germany for a year to
learn German:

When I was about nineteen I left the finishing school, very much against
my will. In those days it was always thought that you must get married, so
I became engaged almost at once. But I had the good sense, even in those
days, to break off my engagement, after a great deal of trouble, and
eventually I married the same man, seven years later. But I'm very glad
that I broke off the original engagement, although it really was very
difficult, because if I had married early I wouldn't have been in England
during the war, and I wouldn't have wanted that.

Judith Lyttelton was one of the few such girls to take a job:

When I went to America, I found a cousin of mine in Washington at the
embassy, where she was a secretary. She told me she actually earned
money, which I'd never heard of anybody doing. I could hardly wait when I
got back to find a secretarial course. The chic one in those days was
something called 'The Triangle', I think, in South Molton Street, and the
course took nine months. But by great good luck, I heard of Miss Trotman
in Victoria Street. Her course took six months but you were pretty dumb if
you didn't get out in five. She did all the parliamentary reporting and was a
byword, wonderful, and wrote in shorthand at I think it was 200 words a
minute. I passed at 120 words a minute. Miss Trotman's course was,
although not working class, for serious people really wanting jobs and not
wanting to hang about in South Molton Street. So we really stuck at it and I

SHOP GIRLS FROM A MILLINERY ESTABLISHMENT ON AN OUTING

passed out in five months. It was very useful. I'm very glad I did it. Then after the season I went out to Teheran, to an uncle who was Ambassador there. I was out there helping him, doing secretarial work unofficially. Then he got me taken on by the Foreign Office and I was an official secretary. I was paid seven pounds a week and we did work hard, but a good time was had by all, except by the British troops who said, 'No more black jam please.' The black jam was caviare. We had it every day we wished, great fat tins of it. They cost the equivalent of thirty-five pence and they were the best Beluga caviare. It was marvellous; I never got tired of it.

Mrs Huxley remembers little difficulty in finding a job before the war.

You could usually get a job; there was no unemployment. Of the ten children in our family, every one did well. I stayed at home for a while, when I left school, and helped my mother; I was about fifteen. Then I went out and became a milliner and I ended up as a buyer in a store in Finchley.

AN ORPHANAGE

We lived in the business at Finchley; the store provided food and rooms. That was quite the thing to do; we left home and we lived in. Office girls didn't do that, but shop girls did. Sometimes, if it was a small place, the girls would live with the family, but bigger shops had their own premises. We had a small salary and our keep. We worked very long hours, eight o'clock in the morning until eight or nine at night, and Saturdays too. But it was great fun, with the other girls. We had a sitting room of our own where we used to knit and sew in the evenings, or just chat, and we could go out in the evenings, but we had to be back by a certain time. Girls didn't work after they married so I stopped working when I married in 1914.

The thing Dora Orr remembers most was being hard up.

My father was Greek; he came from Corfu. He was a quail merchant. He owned three boats and he used to go from place to place, collecting quails. He would bring them all live to England and I can just remember going to his warehouse, in Old Street in London, and seeing a great pit full of feathers and all the women sitting round it, plucking quails for the London trade. Quails were really good, high class, and very popular for dinners and balls. We often had quails to eat. But then I lost my parents in a carriage accident when I was four. The horse bolted and my father was killed; he died almost at once, but my mother lived for about three months. I can't really remember it, but I do remember my mother was suddenly not there. We had no money left us; we had nothing. I went to a

SUFFRAGISTS IN 1913: 'IT WAS BEFORE WOMEN WERE SO MUCH TO THE FORE'

convent in Aberdeen, as a boarder, because the Reverend Mother had been a great friend of Mother's. I was there until I was about ten, but they didn't teach me much up there so I had to come south and live with one of my married brothers, so that I could go to school.

I was quite good at arithmetic, once I started my education in the south. I had a brother-in-law in the Midland Bank, so he got me a job there when I left school. To begin with it was writing cheques, just an ordinary clerk's job, for ten shillings a week. It wasn't difficult to get a job, not really, but of course you *never* bargained – the pay was whatever it was and you could take it or leave it. I worked in Threadneedle Street, in the head office. I liked the Bank very much. It was before women were so much to the fore;

they were kept as clerks and that sort of thing, but I did rise to be a teller, which was quite something.

In London I lived with my two sisters in a flat. We hadn't much money. I had my digs to pay for, and food, and my fares into work. There wasn't much left out of my ten shillings. But we managed; we always had everything. If there was a party we always managed to get a frock, even if it was one of my sisters' evening frocks cut down. That's why, I think, I've always been good at needlework. If I wanted a frock, I had to make it from something else. It was quite a struggle, but we had a jolly good time. We went to a lot of dances, and we went for holidays every year, always, to the sea.

A YOUNG NANNY

After her parents died Catherine Harvey

had to do something. My sister was a schoolteacher and I decided I would be a nanny. I was very fond of children; my children still come to visit me. My father had been an engineer in Motherwell. Motherwell was full of steel works; the steel brought the money in, in those days. I trained in Edinburgh, at the Domestic Science College in Atholl Crescent. I came out fully trained and I had my own nursery right away. When I started work we had big staffs – butler, batman, housemaid, parlourmaid, everything. I was waited on, hand and foot. I didn't have a nurserymaid, there wasn't the room, so all the rest of the staff waited on me. That's why I saw the staff more than most nannies. But the nursery was very separate. I stayed in the nursery all the evening and I was quite pleased to, when the children were in bed. I used to make their clothes, all that smocking. There were two children; their father was a major in the Scots Greys; he was killed in the war. It was very nice being a nanny; I'd do it again, but I don't know what the gentry do now, whether they have staffs. I think if you have a daily woman you're lucky.

In the thriving cities there seems to have been plenty of work for the boys, much of it extremely arduous, including some jobs which would not now be associated with strenuous physical work. Charles Mitchell's father was a baker in Cardiff and he used to help in the bakery before he went to school in the morning.

The dough was all kneaded by hand in a trough and it was very hard work. We boys didn't do that, but we used to cut and shape the rolls and so on. There was no machinery to cut the dough then; there is now. I was offered the chance to stay at school, but I decided to go into the catering business and I started work in a restaurant, and it was hard work there as well. All the goods coming in had to be checked and weighed, even the milk. That came in ten-gallon churns. I had a dipstick to check the milk, because the supplier wouldn't cheat you, but the roundsman might be on the fiddle. I caught one out once; he said they were twelve-gallon churns, but I said there wasn't such a thing as a twelve-gallon churn. When I put in the dipstick, two of the churns were two gallons short. He would have been selling the milk on the side.

Cardiff was very prosperous then, full of people; it was the biggest of the coal ports, exporting the coal from the valleys. They used to bring down coal dust in barges, turn it into briquettes and export it to Egypt, so I was told. There was a lot of poverty too. The docks were very rough. But I loved Cardiff. The shops and the markets were open all the evening until midnight. On a Saturday evening the market used to be packed and to me, a kid, it was so exciting to walk through the central market, which is covered, and has a market upstairs as well, with pets and birds and tropical fish. You could buy a lot of farm produce, real Caerphilly cheese, and what they call laver bread, made out of seaweed. I used to eat that fried, with bacon. Our clientele, in the restaurant, was often theatre people. We had several theatres; Stoll, the music-hall millionaire, lived in

A BAKER

BOYS AT WORK MAKING HERBAL REMEDIES

COUGH LOZENGE FACTORY

Cardiff. In fact there were five or six millionaires and there were some very large houses near the centre. The food was better then. It was all fresh; everything was done properly. We never used bottled sauces or gravy browning, we made our own. It looked like black jack and you kept that to brown the gravy.

Frank Rattey's father

was one of the first to drive the old steam engines. He used to drive round to different farms for the thrashing. Afterwards, he used to look after the pumping engines for the Winchester Water Company. I used to go with him and he used to lift me up and make believe that it was I who had started these great big engines. Of course, we were very poor, we didn't have much, and my parents suggested I should do a paper round to bring in an extra shilling or two.

I used to do a morning round and an evening round, and I used to get 3s. 6d. a week. I can tell you all the papers. There was *The Times*, the *Morning Post*, the *Telegraph*, the *Morning Advertiser*. Then we come to the cheaper papers: the *Mail*, the *News* (afterwards *Chronicle*), the *Mirror*, the *Leader*. In the evening there was the *Globe*, the *Westminster Gazette*, *St James's Gazette*. I used to go round with these papers for Smith and Son – W. H. Smith. Then, when I left school I looked after a little stall in Winchester Barracks and I used to sell to all the Riflemen. I had that stall until my father learned that I had begun to swear and use bad language,

APPRENTICES IN A FORGE

and he apprenticed me as a whitesmith to a firm in Jewry Street; W. H. Stopher. To be a whitesmith we had to learn plumbing, a certain amount of sheet metal work and blacksmith's work. We spent a lot of time re-tinning the old copper stewpans that they used to use in the kitchens, great batches of those. I used to scour them for hours and hours, terrible job, and then the tinsmith used to re-tin them. I was bound, you see, bound to stop there five years. That was about 1910.

'I USED TO PLAY TRUANT'

Without money or education life could be very hard, as many parents realized. They did their best to educate their children. As Elizabeth Franks said:

I used to play truant. I used to play with Charlie Green – we used to play out in the street until about half past two, then we used to go to school and we used to get the cane for being late. But that didn't stop me. I hated school, I went just to please old Mum, but I hated it and I never learned anything. I was always a pretty good writer, but as for sums, I couldn't do sums at all. I can't do sums now. I think the teacher was all right, but she just *had* to cane me, you see. But I had to go at half past two because Mum would say, 'Have you been to school?' and I wouldn't say no to Mum, so I said, 'Yes, I did' – and I had been to school!

A DELIVERY BOY

Father was a bookbinder; he worked in Hatton Garden. In my young days the men worked and had to work — or starved. When I went to work I was fourteen; that was 1901. I had only half a crown a week, and then I got on to piecework. Millinery's a seasonal job, you see. Sometimes you're very slack, so you're put off, you have to go on the Labour Exchange. Well, at the Labour Exchange, if they found me a job I had to take it, I took it whether I liked it or not. We used to walk to work. I walked to Barbican from where we lived, near the Angel. I walked to work and I walked back.

SUPPER DISHES

Mayonaise of Salmon.

Raised Pie.

Lobster Salad.

Cherry Tartlets.

Game Pie.

Fancy Pastry.

Open Tart.

Tomato and Cucumber Salad.

Ratafia Pudding.

Meat Pie.

Never went in a bus. Horse buses they were, in those days. It wasn't really far, not for a youngster, it didn't hurt us. And I remember, Sundays, my brother and I used to walk to Hampstead, dinner time. Whether we walked back I don't remember, but there used to be a horse bus up the hill, and another horse to help it up. We always had to be back by two o'clock, that was dinner time. I don't think it done us any harm.

Opportunities were few for a country girl like Theresa Cox who was born near Sligo, in the west of Ireland.

There were six of us and my father died when I was very young. My mother had quite a struggle and that is for why I never had much schooling. You didn't get much money in those days, not like you do now. I came into the town and went to work when I was bigger. I went into service. I'd never go into service if I had my time again, but in those days there was nothing else for you, you see.

I took my first job when I was twelve. The people were very nice that I worked for and I stayed there until I was about sixteen. I got up in the morning about seven o'clock, went down to lay the table – we had another maid as well – and then I used to go upstairs when they came down to breakfast and get on with the rooms up there. Sometimes I'd have to get some tea leaves to put on the carpet, to lay the dust. And then I used to come down and clear the tables and wash up the breakfast things. There were four in the family where I was. Then I used to do the lunch – come down about twelve o'clock and lay the table. I had had a bit of time to have my breakfast, at about half past eight. There wasn't much sitting down, really. In the afternoon I had a little bit of rest, and then got some tea. And the dinner again at night; they used to have dinner about half past seven. And then the clearing up until about ten or half past, perhaps, and then to bed until the next morning and you started all over again.

MAID-OF-ALL-WORK

Once a month I would have a day off, and on Tuesday I was off from about two o'clock until about ten. On a Sunday I had some time off after about three o'clock. It was hard work for a girl of twelve, really. We used to have a woman sometimes, a daily woman, but you don't get much help from them. There was one other maid, but she left, she had to go home, her parents were taken ill, so I was left on my own.

When I went out at first, I used to work very hard for half a crown a week. But I didn't do that for long. Then I got twelve pounds a year, but that wasn't much, was it? Then it went up to fourteen pounds. If you went to another place you always got a pound or two more. I had to wear a uniform in the morning and a different one, black, in the afternoons. I had to buy my own things, and aprons and all that was very dear. My money was soon gone. In those days you had cuffs, and collars right up to your neck, it didn't matter if it was hot weather or not. And long dresses. It was terrible, really. The lady I worked for used to have a lot of company as well; that was very tiring. She used to have a woman at night to help me. There was always a lot of silver to do, and brass. Service was very hard. I'm glad I'm finished with it now.

I saw my friends occasionally. They'd come and see me, or I'd go to see them sometimes, if I had time. I wouldn't like to go through it again.

Chapter Eight
A WIDER WORLD

ALBERT BALL, VC, THE GREATEST ENGLISH
FLYING PILOT OF THE FIRST WORLD
WAR, KILLED IN 1917

BRITANNIA MOURNING FOR QUEEN VICTORIA

I started work at fourteen, in millinery, and we had to make black hats. I worked in Barbican, then. We made black hats because everybody was wearing them. We had to work on Saturday as well, until four o'clock in the afternoon, making these blinking black hats that everyone was wearing; I remember that. I think it was when Queen Victoria died. (Elizabeth Franks)

Queen Victoria died at Osborne, in the Isle of Wight, on 22 January 1901. Her death cannot have been entirely unexpected, for she was eighty-one and her reign had been the longest in English history, but it seems to have come as a shock. 'When the Nineteenth Century faded out, nobody was heart-stricken.... But at the end of the Victorian Era, who is not conscious of a great blank?' wrote L. F. Austin in the *Illustrated London News*. It felt most odd to sing 'God Save the King' after sixty-four years of 'God Save the Queen' and Austin went on to suggest that there should be a new national anthem.

The point is rather delicate, but I cannot help asking whether public sentiment can sanction the restoration of the anthem to Henry Carey's original composition? Its associations are so solemnly woven with the great personality that has been taken from us that propriety may, to many minds, seem to demand a new anthem rather than the exact strain that

THE QUEEN IN OLD AGE

Carey is believed to have written in the time of George II. This is but one illustration of the way in which the national loss bruises our tenderest fibres.

What did the children think of the Queen? The Dowager Duchess of Devonshire can remember seeing Queen Victoria:

She came to Beaulieu, my grandfather's villa in France. My grandfather used to go out every year and, when I was older, about four or five, I went too. Then the morning came: 'The Queen's coming! The Queen's coming!' So we were ushered into the hall; we all stood there until the door opened and this minute figure came in. Then we curtseyed and she was taken on and given tea. I had a bouquet to give to her, but of course she was dressed in black and looked extremely boring. There was a very dressy lady-in-waiting behind, so I refused to give the flowers to the Queen and insisted on giving them to the lady-in-waiting, who got them in the end – the Queen gave up. I think perhaps she was rather amused; it was an unusual occasion for her. I should have liked to have known her. She must have been a rather wonderful old woman, I think.

Victoria Dane, too young to remember the Queen, had a rather unflattering account of her from her parents:

Father was one of Queen Victoria's ADCs and when my parents came home on leave, if Father was on duty, Mother had to appear too. And, you know, the Queen never allowed *anybody* to sit down, the whole time that she was there. *She* would sit, but everyone else had to stand – even poor, wretched pregnant women. She was an awful old tyrant. Royalty was so absolutely revered; I suppose that was just how it was, in those days.

VILLAGE CELEBRATION OF THE RELIEF
OF MAFEKING, MAY 1900

Not long before the Queen died, there was one memorable night of rejoicing. On 18 May 1900, a Reuter telegram brought the news of the relief of Mafeking, and London went wild with delight and patriotism. The crowds thronged to the Mansion House, where the

NEWS OF THE SOUTH AFRICAN WAR

'INFANT IMPERIALISTS': CHARLES
ROBINSON IN THE *SPHERE*, 1900

Lord Mayor appeared and tried to make his words heard over the
jubilation. 'I wish the music of your cheers could reach Mafeking.
For seven long weary months a handful of men has been besieged
by a horde. We never doubted what the end would be. British pluck
and valour when used in a right cause must triumph.' Baden-
Powell and Lord Roberts were cheered again and again as the news
spread rapidly through Britain and the Empire. There were celebrations in Canada, in Australia, in India, as well as in towns and
villages all over Britain.

Frank Rattey was then a child of four in Winchester.

My father took me in his arms and took me down to see the illuminations
and the torchlight procession. My brother was about twelve years older
than I was; he was there with a girl, and I well remember her taking out a

THE KAISER ARRIVING FOR THE FUNERAL
OF QUEEN VICTORIA

KING AND KAISER IN THE FUNERAL
PROCESSION

rosette, red, white and blue, and in the centre was a picture of Baden-Powell in his scout's hat. She pinned this rosette on me and I was ever so proud, of course. All the recreation ground was illuminated with little fairy lights. There wasn't electricity in those days; it was all candles, in different coloured pots, green and red and blue, and they were all strung round everywhere. It was all one mass of colour.

A new word was coined to describe the behaviour of the crowds – mafficking.

Eight months later the old Queen died. 'I remember the news-papers, with their great black borders.' The funeral was undoub-tedly impressive; the silence of the crowds as the bier passed through the streets of London is remembered by many spectators. 'The silence seemed as though one were looking at vast masses through a glass that prevented sound from coming to the ears', wrote the Duke of Argyll, and Austin wrote; 'When our eyes fell upon the bier there was a hush so deep that you might have thought the hearts of the crowd stood still. There will always linger in my mind a picture of that multitude of bared heads, and white faces rigid with intensity of feeling.'

The Dowager Duchess of Devonshire, then a child of six, stood on a table at a window and watched the procession go by; King Edward VII, the Kaiser, the King of Greece, the King of Portugal, Prince Charles of

THE KING AND THE ROYAL MOURNERS SALUTING AS QUEEN VICTORIA'S COFFIN WAS CARRIED TO THE TRAIN AT PADDINGTON

Denmark, the Grand Duke of Baden, the Crown Prince of Siam, the Duke of Saxony, the Duke of Sparta, Grand Duke Michael of Russia, the Crown Princes of Germany, Denmark, Sweden and Norway, and Rumania, the Archduke Francis Ferdinand of Austria, the King of the Belgians.

I can remember the long string of people, and the gun carriage. I suppose it was a long, long time since they'd had a gun carriage, because of Queen Victoria living so long, and that's why it made such a tremendous impression. I stood there, on a table, and watched this thing go by. I can remember the Kaiser, dressed as a hussar, in black, with a hat, a feathered hat, riding behind. It meant nothing to me, but it's a picture in my mind. I can see it now.

CORONATION BONFIRE, 1902

Edward VII's coronation was to be held in June 1902, but at the last moment the King fell ill and the ceremony had to be postponed. The announcement came too late for an unfortunate journalist of the *Lady's Realm* magazine, calling herself 'A Peer's daughter'. She described the non-existent coronation as a 'never-to-be-forgotten picture' and also unwisely allowed herself some tart comments on the cancelled Gala at the Opera. 'Seldom have we had a worse chorus.... As for Caruso, he is a distinct disappointment.' The coronation was finally held on 9 August 1902.

THE CORONATION OF EDWARD VII

We had sports, and a mug, and a medal with a red, white and blue ribbon on it, pinned on with a safety pin, and there was a march past. We learned songs for the occasion and I well remember one of them, 'The Maple Leaf for Ever'. That was a Canadian song that we sang for the coronation of Edward VII.

In those pre-television days, public events meant little to children unless they were in some way involved. Judith Lyttelton remembers the general elections because her father stood as a Conservative for South Hereford.

He stood for Parliament in 1902, when he was still at the South African War, and, as his chief of staff, who was running his election campaign for him because he was away, told us, 'His absence at the front contributed greatly to his victory' – you can take that both ways, of course! The Liberals got in in 1906, I think it was, and then in 1910 he got back in as MP and remained in. I remember the tremendous excitement of coming out onto the Town Hall steps for the result to be announced. It was thrilling.

THE KING WAS AN ENTHUSIASTIC
MOTORIST

KING EDWARD AT THE RACES

Most children remember little more than half-understood scraps of grown-up conversation – 'My father came in and said "There's been a terrible disaster at sea – the *Titanic* has been shipwrecked."' Or, attracted by the pictures, they would turn over the pages of the *Illustrated London News*. 'All the *Illustrated London News* were kept in our nursery in London, and we used to pore over them endlessly.'

Victoria Dane, in the Sudan, had a royal visitor:

When I was four or five, I was told that a princess was coming. This was when Princess Beatrice came. In those days there was no bridge across the Nile; the train came in to Omdurman and you had to cross the Nile by boat. I was quite used to rather eminent people coming, with their valets and their lady's maids and so on; in those days they used to travel like that, when they came on shooting trips. But this time I had been told that a princess was coming and that I was to give her a bouquet, so I practised my curtsey and all the rest of it. Down we went to Omdurman, and went across in the boat, and in came the train, with all the netting over the windows to try to stop the dust coming in.

But she was as much disappointed with the Princess as the Dowager Duchess of Devonshire had been with her mother, Queen Victoria:

Suddenly out of this train appeared a funny little person. I can see her now, in a black alpaca suit, rather fat and very much pinched in round the middle, with a little black toque on her head. (Royalty were almost always in black in those days because they all went into deep mourning for anybody, any relation, who died.) Anyway, she arrived, and they tried to push me forward, but nothing would make me go. I imagined that a princess would have a crown, and long golden hair, just like the ones in my storybooks; no one had thought of what I would be expecting. So eventually my piping voice was heard to say, 'Where's the Princess? I'm not going to give her flowers to her lady's maid.'

The appearance of the King was familiar, from the newspapers and magazines and from the pictures of him and Queen Alexandra in their coronation robes which hung in many a nursery. Edward was a popular figure. Many can remember the excitement and pleasure when his horse, Minoru, won the Derby in 1909 and was led in by the King himself. When he died in the following year, G. K. Chesterton tried to account for his popularity.

He was the average man enthroned. . . . His popularity in poor families was so frank as to be undignified; he was really spoken of by tinkers and tailors as if he were some gay and prosperous member of their own family.

Some families looked rather askance at their Merry Monarch: 'He did come to Hatfield, but we were all locked up.' However, his relish for life and his homely touch seem to have endeared him to most of

'A GAY AND PROSPEROUS MEMBER OF THEIR OWN FAMILY'

his subjects. Baden-Powell's account of him gives some idea of this:

> After dinner King Edward called me aside and sat me down on the sofa beside him and talked for half an hour about my Boy Scouts. He would like to review the Scouts the following year in Windsor Park.

At Balmoral, Edward tackled Baden-Powell on a subject close to the royal heart:

> I want to speak to you seriously. I have watched you at meals and I notice that you don't eat enough. When working as you are doing you must keep up your system. I am sending with you some venison to tempt you to eat more. Don't forget – eat more.

BLÉRIOT FLIES THE CHANNEL, JULY 1909

SCOUTS, BOTH BOYS AND GIRLS, EDWARDIAN PAPER TOYS

ARTHUR RACKHAM PORTRAIT OF THE KING IN BARRIE'S PETER PAN IN KENSINGTON GARDENS

King Edward's funeral was a splendid occasion. Nine sovereigns followed his coffin: George V, the Kaiser, and the Kings of Norway, Greece, Spain, Denmark, Portugal, Bulgaria and Belgium. In the funeral procession were hussars from Austro-Hungary, Danish hussars, German dragoons, troops from Portugal, Russia and Spain, representatives from the fleets of Germany, Russia, Spain and Sweden. 'The gathering aroused the greatest interest,' commented the *Illustrated London News*, and added ominously, 'If a war were to break out, it would be necessary to seek in this procession of potentates the commanders of the striving military forces.' But such forebodings passed the children by.

We were taken to the procession; we watched it from my father's chambers in Bridge Street, and I can remember the muffled drums. They led the King's charger in the procession with his boots reversed, and they led his terrier, Caesar. The dog wouldn't leave his body when he died. I do remember that the press was very keen on this terrier. But the thing that I remember best was Cossie throwing up the window to hear the newsboys shouting, 'The King is dead,' she said, 'Oh, the King is dead,' and I burst into tears.

EDWARD VII'S FUNERAL

Everyone, including children, wore black arm bands. As Victoria Dane said:

Can you believe it? I was ten years old when King Edward died and I was put into full mourning, a black coat and skirt, until the Court mourning was over. Aged ten! If you were anything official, which Father was, you had to go into full mourning, black lines round the writing paper and all that sort of thing, and the children had to, too.

After Edward's death the department stores were thronged with women buying black mourning clothes, which was why a royal death meant little more than hard work to a milliner like Elizabeth Franks.

'I AM CAESAR, AND BELONG TO THE KING'

COVER OF *THE ILLUSTRATED LONDON NEWS* MAY, 1910

The following year, 1911, there was the coronation of George V and as Judith Lyttelton's father was in the House of Commons, she and her family had seats just opposite Buckingham Palace:

I have that memory very distinctly. The seats were banked right up around the Victoria Memorial so we could see everything. What we thought of George V I don't know, but of course everyone enjoys coronations so just then he was very popular, and everyone adored Queen Alexandra; she looked too beautiful for words.

Coronation year was remarkable for its long, hot summer. The highest temperatures in London were recorded on 9 August; 97° in the shade at 4 p.m. at Kensington, and 100° at Greenwich. This was a record for London, while July and August were the hottest months since records had begun fifty-four years previously.

Frank Rattey remembers George V and Queen Mary coming to Winchester, to the cathedral thanksgiving celebrations of 1912.

They had to underpin the cathedral at Winchester because it was slipping. It was built like on a raft in the water-meads which are all around there. The money was terrific; £750,000, I think it was, and that was a lot of money in those days. They'd had a public subscription and a pageant to raise contributions. I remember the King coming, and I remember there was a diver employed there, a man of the name of Walker, a Londoner, and he could drink beer like I don't know what. He'd go down and lay the cement. It wasn't fresh water down there, it was all dark and cloudy and stagnant, and this man Walker spent years down there. They made a statue of the diver and that's still in Winchester cathedral, because he absolutely saved that building.

DIVER WALKER, WHO SAVED WINCHESTER CATHEDRAL

GEORGE V AND QUEEN MARY AT THE WINCHESTER CATHEDRAL THANKSGIVING, 1912

In 1914, another golden summer, my father was at a private school in Oxford.

The summer term ended in July, and when I came back I can't in the least remember that there was any excitement, although it must have been boiling up. But I do remember this, that we went to church at St Mary's, Graham Street, and the sermon that was preached there at the end of July 1914 was all about the awful peril of civil war in Ireland. That was what everybody was preoccupied with at that time; it wasn't until about 1 August that the European crisis began to take possession of the headlines. Of course I don't remember any of that, but I do remember my brother, John, coming up to where we slept, right at the top of the house. He was thirteen or fourteen, then, and stayed down for dinner. Anyway, he came up and he said, 'It's very exciting; there's going to be a war,' and I said, 'Oh!' or something – I don't think there was any particular alarm.

In Winchester, Frank Rattey heard the garrison bugles summoning the reservists.

Being a garrison town, there were a lot of reservists all round. They knew war was imminent and Winchester Barracks was crowded with men. I remember the day that war was declared, the Rifles marching along Station Hill with fixed bayonets, and as they marched they were shouting, 'We'll give them German sausage!' I've often thought of that. They were so pleased to think they were going to have a go at the Jerries, but I've often thought, 'How many of them poor chaps came back?' They were the first to go. We called them 'The Contemptible Army', but no doubt about it, they were soldiers.

The Boy Scouts leaped into action. Baden-Powell's first step

was to get all bridges, railway culverts, telegraph and cable lines, waterworks, etc., guarded by posses of Scouts, thereby to counter any attempts by nearly 100,000 domiciled Germans from interfering with our communications. The boys mobilized at once... took up their guarding duties with the greatest keenness... the coastguard service was taken over by Boy Scouts, under a few Naval POs, from John O'Groats to the Land's End.

The guarding duties were soon taken over by Territorials, but Scouts continued to act as coastguards until the Armistice.

My father remembered that there were the most absurd spy scares:

There was a man in the village who was very keen on spies – he even thought my uncle was a spy, when he arrived at the station on his way to stay with us. Cowden Station was thought to be a place where sabotage was almost bound to occur. Everyone was prevailed upon to join the Special Constables, and they had three or four people guarding the railway bridge at Cowden Station, which must have been very low, I should have thought, among the enemy's objectives. There were the milk trains through Cowden, and there was a signalman who used to go out on his balcony and ring a little bell when he let the train into his section, so as

A SUGGESTION FOR ENJOYING THE CORONATION OF GEORGE V

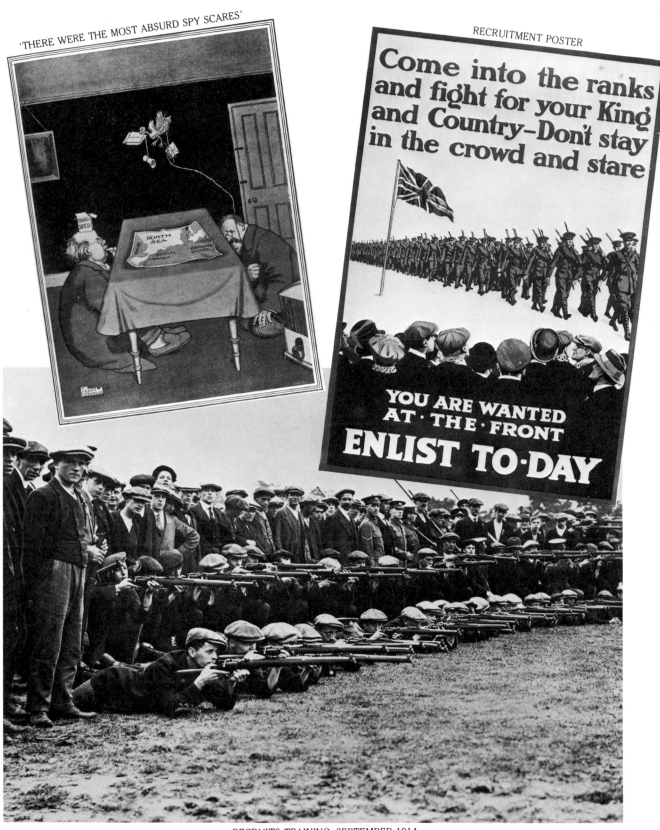

'THERE WERE THE MOST ABSURD SPY SCARES'

Come into the ranks
and fight for your King
and Country–Don't stay
in the crowd and stare

YOU ARE WANTED
AT · THE · FRONT
ENLIST TO·DAY

RECRUITS TRAINING, SEPTEMBER 1914

you walked along you could hear the bell and, if you wanted to catch the train, you quickened your steps. I don't think that they kept up the guard on Cowden Station for very long – 'Business as Usual' was the slogan. When I went back to school, German spies were a great thing. We went solemnly to the headmaster to tell him that we thought he ought to know that a very suspicious character had been seen at the end of the playing fields; undoubtedly he was a German spy. Anyone at all who was unfamiliar was thought to be a spy.

What I remember most about 1914 was the tremendous enthusiasm [said Catherine Staples]. We were at war! My brother was so excited and thrilled about it that he actually joined up on the day before war was declared, as a trooper. He got into a regiment afterwards. We were all full of patriotism and enthusiasm; I don't remember any horror of what was to come. The Second War was worse, because one was old enough to realize how futile it all was.

In Scotland Mabel Walker

heard them all whispering, 'There's going to be a war,' before it came, and 'What's going to happen to us?' The enlistment offices were springing up everywhere and you got a shilling if you joined up. The soldiers were

'THE TREMENDOUS ENTHUSIASM' OF 1914

parading through the streets, the Gordon Highlanders, and one school was turned into a hospital. But I was only thirteen. I never really noticed all my cousins going to the war, because I wasn't really attached to them like I was to my girl cousins. The boys were never there when I visited my aunts; they were always out at the time I used to visit, in the early evening.

Nevertheless the war changed her life completely:

All the fishermen went to the war, and there was no herring industry at all. So my father lost practically all his money, because the fishermen were the people who were keeping his business alive. We had to leave Fraserburgh and go to Aberdeen, where I went to the girls' high school.

'By that time we were just cannon fodder and they weren't interested in teaching us; there was no point,' remembers one who was then a boy at Winchester, while my father, also at Winchester, recalls his brother talking to a friend in the dormitory at night.

JOHN TRAVERS 'BOY' CORNWELL, VC, SIXTEEN-YEAR-OLD HERO OF THE BATTLE OF JUTLAND

VADS IN A SMALL AUXILIARY HOSPITAL, 1914

'They were talking about how long they had to live. They were quite aware that they would probably be dead shortly after leaving school.'

Those girls who were old enough did voluntary work in hospital and elsewhere.

Lady Roberts ran the Red Cross hospital for the Tommies in Ascot [said Lady Remnant]. I was still at school, but I used to work there in the holidays. I used to bicycle off to the hospital and I scrubbed the floors and washed the paint and polished the brass. There was one terrible day when I was supposed to be going up to London afterwards. I'd finished my job and I'd brought my things to change into and I was just going off to catch the train when the matron came in and she said, 'Did you put ammonia in the water when you washed the paint?' and I hadn't. So she said, 'Well, you must do it all again,' and I had to.

'MY DAD'S AT THE FRONT – WHERE IS YOURS?'

Dora Orr, then about fifteen, washed up dishes in a convalescent home. 'My sister went with me. We went into the kitchen, and there the plates were, piled high, all the plates for the day. We used to wash up the whole evening.'

Catherine Staples helped in a hospital in Endell Street, just by Covent Garden:

It was a hospital that was run entirely by women surgeons and doctors; Dr Elizabeth Garrett Anderson's daughter, Louisa, was the head surgeon. There were six hundred men in that hospital. One of my duties was that I had the keys, and if an air-raid warning went I had to go and unlock all the doors that let people out. In those days, an air-raid warning meant Boy Scouts going along the road shouting, 'Take cover! Take cover!' and

LONDON: SOLDIERS COMING HOME ON LEAVE

policemen ringing bells. Well, I had a good opportunity to get out on the roof and see what I could see. One night I went out on the roof – and I saw a Zeppelin! But I can't tell you much about it, because I was so frightened that I quickly went indoors again. It dropped a bomb on *John Bull*'s offices, just at the end of Endell Street, and the whole thing came through and killed a hundred and twenty people. The vicar of St Paul's, Covent Garden, had a shelter there for his people and they were all killed under there, or most of them. It was so amazing that the Army didn't shoot down the beastly thing. I suppose in those days they didn't have the right kind of

THE NEW YEAR, A CARTOON OF 1915

WALKING TO THE RAILWAY STATION
WITH AN UNCLE (MAXFIELD PARRISH
FROM *THE GOLDEN AGE*)

guns. The Zeppelins were such a huge size, and they moved quite slowly, so far as I remember. To think that they could come sailing over London and no one could knock them down! It seems so strange.

Always there were fathers and brothers leaving for the front:

I remember 1914 so well. My father had just come back on leave from India when war broke out and of course he went straight back. He left by train to catch the boat to India, and I remember the railway station, masses of men everywhere, everyone pushing their own luggage.

Judith Lyttleton's father was wounded at least twice;

he was always back home, either on leave, or wounded, or both. He managed to acquire two great brass shells, and they were polished and put one on each side of the stairs of our house in Chester Street. He was killed in 1918 and my mother was left with us five.

It was a very sad time [said Dora Rees]. All the men in our village, which was a colliery village near Swansea, practically all of them went to the war, unless they were needed for the colliery. I had three brothers in the war; two in India and one in the navy.

I knew lots of boys that never came back [said Elizabeth Franks]. My brother was wounded in the war; that's why he didn't live so long. He was blown up, on a transport, and he was never really well after. He went to work, but he was never right.

Frank Rattey, at eighteen, was old enough to join up.

I got clothed there, at Winchester Castle; great big army boots, with iron studs in – of course, I couldn't manage them. My mother and my sister and sister-in-law came to say goodbye, and I was so pleased, I made to run and ended up on my behind because of those boots. We went to train on the sands at Bournemouth and then under canvas at Romsey. That was the first time I'd ever been to a church service, and I felt so proud, dressed as a soldier, with my bayonet, you know. But when I got inside it was 'You, you and you – go and blow the organ!' So nobody could see me.'

Then they said, 'You're for India. You're to take over from the regular army in India and look after the frontier.' Of course, we were raw recruits. We went on the SS *Shropshire*, a converted meat vessel, a big ship. We were slung up in hammocks, eighteen inches apart, down in the hold. From Gibraltar, Japanese destroyers took us over; they escorted us through. Just outside Malta, the alarm went. We scrambled up a staircase to our positions, and we waited with our rafts to see if we had to jump, but the Japanese got us into Malta and there we had to wait. The German submarines were after us – there'd been a French transport ship sunk just ahead of us. The Japanese Navy were smart lads, no doubt about it. They got us into Malta, and then they took us on to Port Said.

It was terrible doing guard at night. The stench used to be awful. I suppose the temperature up top must have been over 100 degrees. They used to sling a great canvas funnel from the mast, to bring air into the hold. If you were on guard, you had to go down there to see that nobody was smoking; I used to dread it. Some of the soldiers died of heat stroke. A pal of mine, he died. It wasn't till we got into the Canal that they let us sleep on deck. You can tell what sort of journey we had. Then we only had one suit of drill khaki, and after re-coaling the ship was as black as the ace of spades. You can guess what we looked like. When we got to Bombay, the first thing we all did was to try to get some soap and water to wash our things. We were in Bombay for some time. There were showers at the barracks – it was a godsend. Nobody seemed to know that we were there and for some days we had nothing to eat but bananas and bread with ants in it.

MODEL OF A BRITISH OFFICER – BUT MADE IN GERMANY, ABOUT 1914

The surprising thing about the war is how small the impact was on families not directly involved; those with fathers too old, sons too young, to join up. There are no uniforms to be seen in my father's photograph albums; only in a group of stout Belgian lady exiles, planting a commemorative tree in the park, and two beaming cousins, children, captioned 'Zeppelin refugees', are reminders of the war.

Governesses produced maps and little flags, which the children moved about to show the positions of the armies; the very superior German toys vanished from the shops; horses and servants were in short supply. Perhaps the shortage of horses was the most obvious to the children.

'BUSINESS AS USUAL' – PRAMS, TOYS AND TEMPORARY WAR BUILDINGS IN REGENT'S PARK, LONDON

There was a lamentable tendency, when someone arrived at the station, not to send a luggage cart down. One of us children would be commissioned to meet the train. When my great-uncle came, it was quite something, because he was an enormously tall man, a great talker and very lame. He would put his hand on your shoulder to steady himself and he would stop from time to time, when he was developing a point, and you were pushed about to emphasize it. Very painful. This was as a result of the war, when horses, and carts and carriages were much reduced. If it was wet, or dark, then they would send somebody down to meet the train, but otherwise the children went.

PEACE CELEBRATIONS, LONDON, 1919

Over the Channel, the men were singing:

I want to go home,
I want to go home.
I don't want to go to the trenches no more,
Where the Whizz-bangs and Johnsons do rattle and roar.
Take me right over the sea
Where the Allemande can't bayonet me.
Oh my!
I don't want to die.
I want to go home.

But in England it was 'Business as Usual' and, later, Mary Clive wrote in *A Day of Reckoning*:

I think I am right in saying that to the end people remained, incredible as it may seem, extraordinarily *jolly*.

EPILOGUE

FOUR ROYAL GENERATIONS: QUEEN
VICTORIA, EDWARD VII, GEORVE V AND
EDWARD VIII

'Is It You' appeared in an anthology of suitable pieces for boys to recite, published in 1903. Whether the poem was a popular choice with performers is open to doubt, but it is an admirable summing up of the Edwardian code of honour, integrity and self-sacrifice, oddly and typically mingled with baths, fresh air, dull food and early rising.

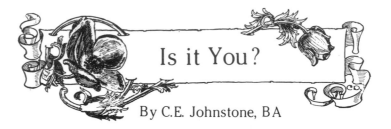

Is it You?

By C.E. Johnstone, BA

Here are portraits of some youngsters that I knew:
Does the Reader feel like fitting on the shoe?
    For each subject of this poem
    Is a real boy – I still know him.
    And I wonder if by any chance it's YOU.

I used to know a boy who always lay in bed till eight.
Then scamped his tub and tore into his clothes at fearful rate,
And remarked, when he came down, 'I didn't know it was so late!'
    Was it you – this sleepy sluggard? Was it you?

Another boy is up and out as soon as it is light;
He loves to bathe before the sun has put the day to flight:
And then he'll fish till breakfast (though he seldom gets a bite!).
    Is it you – this early bather? Is it you?

I knew a boy who fussed about the things he had to eat;
He grumbled at the pudding and he growled about the meat;
With his cup half full of sugar he would whine, 'It isn't sweet!'
    Was it you – this dainty feeder? Was it you?

His cousin just took everything exactly as it came;
Roast turkey, resurrection pie, he ate it just the same;
Never quarrelled with his victuals – didn't think it was 'the game'.
    Was it you – this healthy youngster? Was it you?

And every day this very boy would get into a scrape,
But he never shirked the consequence, however bad its shape:
Always stayed to face the music – left the others to escape.
    Was it you – this plucky scapegrace? Was it you?

There was another kind of boy who loved 'to have a lark',
Provided he was pretty sure that he could 'keep it dark';
But when found out he shuffled! Sense of honour? Not a spark!
   Was it you – this shifty coward? Was it you?

I knew a boy who 'thought it grand' to gamble and to bet;
He'd talk about the Derby and the latest prize-ring pet;
I think he was the dullest kind of youth I ever met!
   Was it you – this silly 'sportsman'? Was it you?

Another boy was reckoned as a thorough little brick;
For hardship, pain, or danger – well, he didn't care a stick;
But there was one thing that he funked – he dared not 'go on tick'.
   Was it you – this canny thriftster? Was it you?

It once was my misfortune to know a certain boy
Whose coming home for holidays was not a source of joy,
For he used to tease his sisters and the servants to annoy.
   Was it you – this doubtful blessing? Was it you?

He too possessed a cousin of a very different brand:
'When Jack comes home again next week,' they said, 'it will be grand!
For he always gives his mother and the girls a helping hand.'
   Is it you – this useful brother? Is it you?

I knew a boy who promised well and made a splendid start,
But tired of the narrow path and chose the crooked part;
His name is never mentioned now. He broke his mother's heart.
   Was it you – this weak-kneed stripling? Was it you?

I know a man that gave his life his fellow men to free
From slavery and sin and want, for neither fame nor fee;
And I heard a voice that whispered, 'Thou hast done it unto Me.'
   Is it you – this noble worker? Is it you?

Unless otherwise stated the photographs which appear in this book are part of the John Topham Picture Library or the author's private collection.

Baby: *Popperfoto*
Motor bus: *London Transport Board*
Boys wore sailor hats: *Andrew Pitcairn-Knowles Gallery*
The effort of running a house: *Kodak Museum*
Teatime: *Andrew Pitcairn-Knowles Gallery*
Leaning over the bridge: *Kodak Museum*
Match seller: *Kodak Museum*
Keeping London clean: *Kodak Museum*
Buy my pretty flowers: *Kodak Museum*
Botany class: *Greater London Council*
Winchester College: *Hampshire County Library*
Spare the brush: *Mansell Collection*
A family outing: *Andrew Pitcairn-Knowles Gallery*
Aware of the empire: *National Army Museum*
Washing doll's clothes: *Kodak Museum*
Playing diabolo: *Andrew Pitcairn-Knowles Gallery*
Hats on the beach: *Kodak Museum*
Telephone exchange: *Manchester Local History Library*
A street organ: *Popperfoto*
Derby day (2 pictures): *Andrew Pitcairn-Knowles Gallery*
Family at the races: *Andrew Pitcairn-Knowles Gallery*
Flying at Hendon: *London Transport Executive*
'At home': *Kodak Museum*
Enthusiasm of 1914: *Kodak Museum*
The Navy: *Imperial War Museum*
Shop girls: *Popperfoto*
An orphanage: *Press Association*
Suffragists: *Press Association*
A baker: *Kodak Museum*
News of the South African war: *Kodak Museum*
Albert Ball: *Imperial War Museum*
King Edward VII in a motor car: Coronation of King Edward VII: *Reproduced by gracious permission of Her Majesty the Queen*
Portrait of the King: *Arthur Rackham, from J. M. Barrie's 'Peter Pan in Kensington Gardens', Hodder and Stoughton*
Diver Walker: *Hampshire Country Library*